FINGERPRINT
Classification and
Interpretation
SIMPLIFIED

Third Edition

Billie F. Scott

Custom Publishing

New York   Boston   San Francisco
London   Toronto   Sydney   Tokyo   Singapore   Madrid
Mexico City   Munich   Paris   Cape Town   Hong Kong   Montreal

Printed in the United States of America

10 9 8 7 6 5 4 3 2 1

2009420252

JP

**Pearson
Custom Publishing**
is a division of

www.pearsonhighered.com

ISBN 10: 0-558-32121-6
ISBN 13: 978-0-558-32121-5

Contents

Various shapes of lines as related to pattern formation
Terms used to identify characteristics

LOOP   ARCH   WHORL
a. Radial   a. Plain   a. Plain whorl
b. Ulnar   b. Tented   b. Central pocket loop
                                c. Double loop whorl
                                d. Accidental whorl

Illustrations of difficult and unusual patterns

Divisions of the Henry formula explained
Pattern codes for blocking out a fingerprint card

About the Author

Billie Scott has worked in the field of fingerprints for more than 35 years while employed at both the Los Angeles Sheriff and Los Angeles Police Departments. During her career, Ms Scott conducted over 9,000 crime scene investigations, completed fingerprint analyses that resulted in more than 100,000 positive identifications and worked in conjunction with the FBI on bank robbery investigations. When she retired from the LAPD she held the position of forensic print specialist. She also qualified as an expert prosecution witness in juvenile, municipal, superior and federal courts.

Ms Scott received specialized training from the FBI in Deceased and Disaster Identification and Advanced Latent Fingerprint Techniques. She attended the California Criminalistic Institute and has a certificate in Court Presentation of Evidence.

Ms Scott has been an instructor of Fingerprint Classification in the Los Angeles Unified School District and Community College System since 1982.

Dedication

To my husband, Sylvester Scott, my children: LaVonne, Robert, James, and Ebbins. My grandchildren: Lawrence, Siobhan, and Donna.

Acknowledgments

I wish to express my appreciation to the Federal Bureau of Investigation, United States Department of Justice, for the use of material and diagrams from their publication, *The Science of Fingerprints*.

Thanks to the following:

Ebbins Harris, my daughter, who worked meticulously for many hours to help me present this book in an excellent manner.

Debra Renfro, my dear friend, who constantly nudged me to get started on this book. Her confidence in me was very inspiring.

Special thanks to Drs. Fred and Betty Price, my shining examples. Dr. Fred inspired me with his teaching method that I have successfully applied in presenting information in a way that is easily understood.

Introduction

This book is directed to the beginning student of the science of fingerprints and gives detailed instructions on how to interpret fingerprint patterns and classify a set of fingerprints using the Henry system of classification. Every effort has been made to present the material in this book in a way that will be easily understood. The basic rules and definitions of the science are shown in italics and are followed by a detailed explanation in laymen's terms.

For many years students have had difficulty understanding the various books that have been published regarding fingerprints. Many of them are written to be used as reference manuals for law enforcement officers and agencies. The information in this book is outlined in such a way that student and instructor will be able to follow each phase of classification and interpretation without becoming confused.

Fingerprints are distinctive ridge outlines which appear on the inside of the end joints of the fingers and thumbs. The words "ridges" and "lines" are used interchangeably and mean the same thing in the science of fingerprints. These ridges have definite shapes, which are called "characteristics" and make up what we call a "pattern." The interpretation of a pattern is determined by the type and shape of the characteristics. Only the end joints are used to classify prints to arrive at a formula. The formula is called the Henry Classification system and was developed in 1901 by Sir Edward Richard Henry, Assistant Commissioner, London Metropolitan Police. This system enabled fingerprints to be easily filed, searched, and traced against thousands of others. Today it is referred to as the Henry system, which is a formula assigned to a set of ten fingerprints.

In past years, the Henry system was used primarily to classify fingerprints. When a suspect was initially arrested, a set of fingerprints was taken and placed on a card. The suspect's case history was established and filed in the Identification Unit's master records. Upon each subsequent arrest, a new set of prints was taken and searched manually to determine if there was a prior arrest. In order to search accurately the technician had to know how to compare the characteristics of prints to arrive at a positive identification.

Of all the methods of identification, fingerprinting has proved to be the most accurate and dependable. To this date no two individuals have been found to have identical fingerprints. Modern technology has developed the means to expedite the process of searching for prints using the Automated Fingerprint System (AFIS). Many law enforcement agencies use different computerized systems, but each one is designed to make the searching process simpler.

In the present day law enforcement procedures, a suspect's prints are stored in a computer database, which then provides a list of possible matches. Although computers are very efficient, the human eye is needed to make the final decision as to positive identification for complete accuracy. This is why a thorough knowledge of the interpretation and comparison of fingerprints is needed.

CHAPTER I

Fingerprint Characteristics Defined

Ridges used in fingerprint classification are raised lines that appear on the inside of the end joints of the fingers and thumbs.

Pattern is the name assigned to fingerprints on each finger and is determined by the way the lines are shaped.

Pattern Area is located in the centermost part of the fingerprint itself and should be the initial focus for determining ridge count and pattern interpretation. The examiner's eyes should immediately concentrate on the center area of the pattern in order to analyze it.

Impression is an imprint of a finger that has been placed on a fingerprint card. The term is used interchangeably with the word "fingerprint."

Ending Ridge is a ridge that enters the pattern and stops in mid-air. It may be shaped vertically or horizontally. These ridges are not connected to any other ridge. *An ending ridge does not complete a continuous flow in the pattern area.* Notice the pattern illustration in Figure 1. The ridges are flowing continuously, which means they curve and continue going until stopping on the same side they entered. To further explain the entrance of the ridges, the bottom of the print is the area the ridges entered and may be described as the "open end." At the top of the print you will notice ridges curving and continuing to go in a certain direction. These ridges are considered to be completing a continuous flow.

Short Ridge is longer than a dot. Although it is in itself an ending ridge, it may be identified by the mere fact that it is "short" and very noticeable.

Recurving ridge simply means a ridge that curves back on itself.

Shoulders are the point at which the recurving ridge definitely turns inward or curves. They are at the top portion of the recurving ridge and are very important as they indicate the direction in which to count ridges. (Count upwards toward the shoulders.) The lines marked X in Figures 5 to 7 are illustrations of shoulders.

Appendage is an attachment or connection on the outside of a recurving ridge between the shoulders and at right angles (Figures 2, 3, 4; 8-15).

Sufficient Recurve is that part of a ridge between the shoulders that is free of appendages abutting (touching) on the outside at a right angle. If an attachment to a recurve flows off smoothly it is not an appendage.

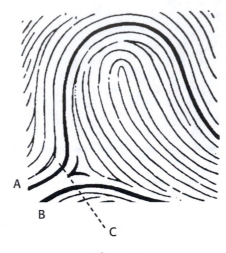

Figure 1

A sufficient recurve may also be called a "smooth" recurve. A sufficient recurve is needed in order to locate a core for counting purposes. Care should be taken to locate the recurve that does not have an appendage.

Spoiled Recurve refers to a recurve with an appendage (connection) on the outside between the shoulders at a right angle. See Figures 8 to 15.

Angles are formed by the meeting of two ridges at a right angle and resemble the letter V. In Figure 16A the ridges marked A and B form an angle.

Island is the expansion of one ridge into two and the rejoining into one ridge again. An island is also referred to as an "enclosure" (Figure 16).

Bifurcation is the dividing of a single ridge into two or more branches. This characteristic is similar to a tree branch and may branch out in any direction (Figure 17).

Divergence is the spreading apart of two lines which have been running parallel or nearly parallel. Lines turn away from each other when diverging (Figure 17).

Figure 2

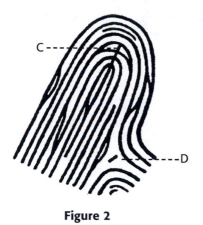

Figure 4

Figure 6

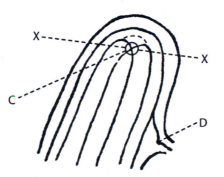

Figure 3

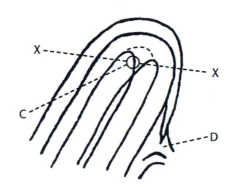

Figure 5

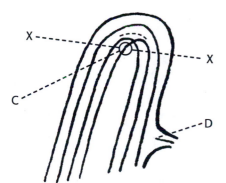

Figure 7

Figure 8

Figure 9

Figure 10

Figure 11

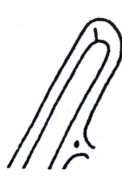

Figure 12

Figure 13

Figure 14

Figure 15

1. SHORT RIDGE

2. ⎫
3. ⎭ BIFURCATION

4. ⎫
5. ⎭ BIFURCATION

6. RIDGE

7. ENDING RIDGE

8. ⎫
9. ⎭ BIFURCATION

10. RIDGE

11. ENDING RIDGE

12. RIDGE

13. SHORT RIDGE

14. ⎫
15. ⎭ BIFURCATION

16. ⎫
17. ⎭ ISLAND

18. ⎫
19. ⎭ BIFURCATION

20. ENDING RIDGE

21. DOT

22. RIDGE

23. ⎫
24. ⎭ ISLAND

25. ENDING RIDGE

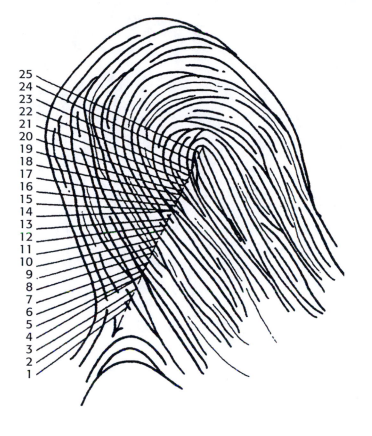

Figure 16

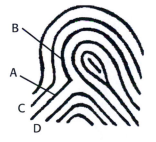

Figure 16A

CHAPTER II

Pattern Types and Their Interpretation

The proper interpretation of fingerprint patterns is very important in order to classify fingerprints and assign the correct coding for computer input. As explained earlier the Henry System of Classification refers to a formula applied to a set of ten fingerprints for the purpose of personal identification.

There are three main groups of patterns: Loops, Arches, and whorls The patterns are divided into sub-groups. These divisions are as follows:

I. LOOP (65%)   **II.** ARCH (5%)   **III.** WHORL (30%)

  a. Radial loop   **a.** Plain arch   **a.** Plain whorl

  b. Ulnar loop   **b.** Tented arch   **b.** Central pocket loop whorl

    1. Angular type   **c.** Double loop whorl

    2. Upthrust   **d.** Accidental whorl

    3. Loop type

In order to interpret the different patterns, it is necessary to learn the definition of each one. The most common pattern of all is the loop. 65% of all fingerprints are loops.

THE LOOP

A loop is that type of fingerprint pattern in which one or more of the ridges enter on either side of the impression, recurve, touch or pass an imaginary line drawn from the delta to the core, and terminate or tend to terminate on or toward the same side of the impression from where it entered. (Figures 35 to 58)

The definition of a loop can be summarized in the list of essentials below:

  a. A sufficient recurve

  b. A delta

  c. A ridge count across a looping ridge (This is determined when the imaginary line from delta to core crosses at least one recurve.)

The recurve must pass in front of the delta in a loop pattern. Once the recurve without an appendage is found the core is chosen.

In order to evaluate a loop or any other pattern in classification, the center or the fingerprint is the starting point. The characteristics in this area will help to determine what the pattern is. Descriptions of the characteristics within a loop are explained below:

Innermost sufficient recurve is the centermost recurve that is free of appendages touching on the outside of the recurve at a right angle.

Looping ridge is a ridge that enters a fingerprint, curves and exits on the same side from which it entered. The looping ridge in a loop is referred to as a recurve.

Focal points are delta and core appearing in the pattern area.

Type lines are the two innermost ridges which start parallel, diverge, surround or tend to surround the pattern area. "Tend to surround" means that a line or lines appear to surround but do not completely enclose the pattern area. The direction of the lines must clearly indicate this.

Type lines are not always two continuous ridges and are often broken. When there is a definite break in a type line, the ridge directly below it is considered its continuation (Figure 18). Type lines may be very short (Figure 19). An angular formation may never be used as a type line. In Figure 16A the ridges marked C and D are type-lines.

The two forks of a bifurcation may never be used as type lines. The exception is when the forks run parallel after bifurcating and then diverge. In this case the two forks become the two innermost as required in the definition and are the type lines as in Figure 20. In Figure 17 the difference between a divergence and bifurcation is shown.

The delta is that point on a ridge nearest the center of the divergence of the type lines. A delta may be: a bifurcation, an abrupt ending ridge, a short ridge, a meeting of two ridges or a point on the first recurving ridge. The delta should never be placed in an empty space but on a ridge as the definition indicates. When there is no ridge between the type lines, the delta is placed on the first recurving ridge.

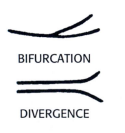

BIFURCATION

DIVERGENCE

Figure 17

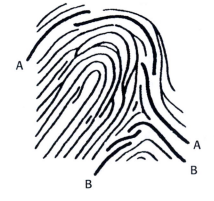

Figure 18

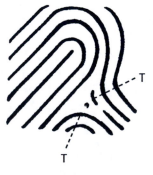

Figure 19

Delta Rules:

- *The delta may not be located at a bifurcation that does not open toward the core.*

- *When there is a choice between a bifurcation and another type of delta, equally close to the point of divergence, the bifurcation is selected.* Notice in Figure 21, the dot A and the bifurcation are equally close to the divergence of the type lines, but the bifurcation is selected as the delta. The ridges marked "T" are the type lines.

- *When there is a series of bifurcations opening toward the core at the point of divergence of the two type-lines, the bifurcation nearest the core is chosen (*Figure 24*)*

- *The delta may not be located in the middle of a ridge running between the typelines toward the core, but at the nearer end only.* If the ridge is entirely within the pattern area, the delta is located at the end nearest the point of divergence of the type lines. If the ridge enters the pattern area from a point below the divergence of the type lines the delta is located at the end nearest the core (Figures 22 and 23).

Figure 20

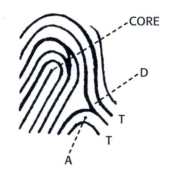

Figure 21

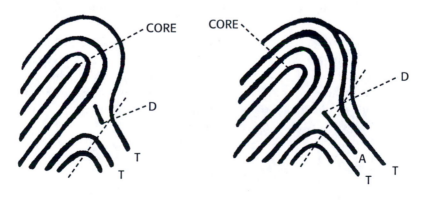

Figure 22

Figure 23

Core is placed on or in the innermost recurve. *Innermost refers to the recurve that* is closest to the center area of the pattern. The lines within the sufficient recurve are called "rods" and are used for core placement. The ridge used for the core is not always in a straight line. The lines within the innermost recurve may be curved.

The following rules apply to core placement:

- *When the innermost sufficient recurve contains no ending rod or ridge rising as high as the shoulders of the loop, the core is placed on the shoulder farthest from the delta* (Figure 24).

- *If both shoulders are equal distance to the delta, the core is located on the center of the sufficient recurve* (Figure 31).

- *When the innermost sufficient recurve contains an uneven number (1, 3, 5) of rods rising as high as the shoulders, the core is placed upon the end of the center rod whether it touches the looping ridge or not.*

- *When the innermost sufficient recurve contains an even number (2, 4, 6) of rods rising as high as the shoulders, the core is placed upon the end of the farther one of the two center rods; that is, the farthest one from the delta.*

Figures 24 to 30 show the delta and core of a series of loops. In Figure 30 there are two rods but "A" does not come up as high as the shoulder line X so B is the core. Figure 5, 6, 7 show interlocking loops at the center. In all these examples two loops are considered as one with two rods inside.

Ridge Counting

The number of ridges intervening between the delta and the core is known as the ridge count. Ridge counting is primarily assigned to loops. If a set of fingerprints has no loops and the other patterns are all whorls, a whorl count may be used. In order to determine the ridge count the fingerprint technician will count each ridge that touches or crosses an imaginary line drawn from delta to core. *Incipient* ridges within a pattern area are ridges that are visibly thinner and less developed than the other ridges. They are not counted in the ridge count. Dots are counted if they are as thick and heavy as the other ridges in the immediate pattern. Both sides of an island or bifurcation are counted.

It is very important to locate the correct delta and core, or an incorrect ridge count will result. *A White space must intervene between the delta and the first ridge count.* If no space exists the first ridge is disregarded. In Figures 32 and 33 the first ridge after the space is counted. In Figure 34, it is not counted because there is no space between it and the delta. The imaginary line is drawn diagonally toward the shoulders. Neither delta nor core is counted. A fingerprint examiner counts each ridge which crosses or touches an imaginary line. Figures 35 to 58 are examples of ridge counts

A two point margin in ridge counting is allowed due to the possibility of visual misinterpretation, distortion or poor condition of the ridge detail. The determination of either a high or low position of the shoulders can result in a difference of one or two counts. The final and key are considered control figures for searching prints. Of the prints within any group classification, only those prints are examined which have a final within 2 ridge counts on each side of the final of the print being searched. If the print to be searched has a final of 14, all prints with a final of 12 through 16 will be compared with it.

Figure 24

Figure 25

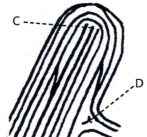

Figure 26

Figure 27

Figure 28

Figure 29

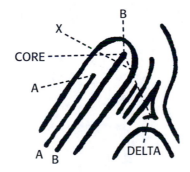

Figure 30

Figure 31

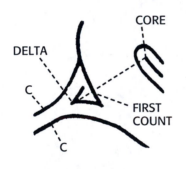

Figure 32

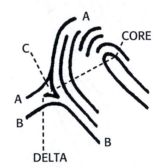

Figure 33

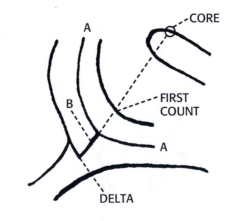

Figure 34

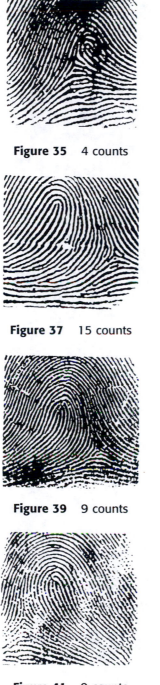

Figure 35   4 counts

Figure 36   7 counts

Figure 37   15 counts

Figure 38   16 counts

Figure 39   9 counts

Figure 40   3 counts

Figure 41   9 counts

Figure 42   20 counts

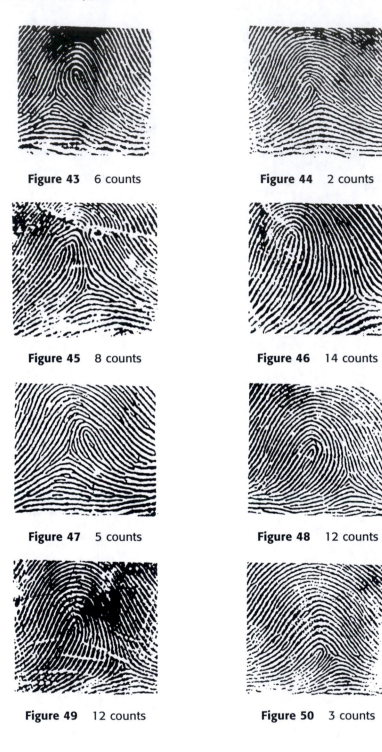

Figure 43   6 counts

Figure 44   2 counts

Figure 45   8 counts

Figure 46   14 counts

Figure 47   5 counts

Figure 48   12 counts

Figure 49   12 counts

Figure 50   3 counts

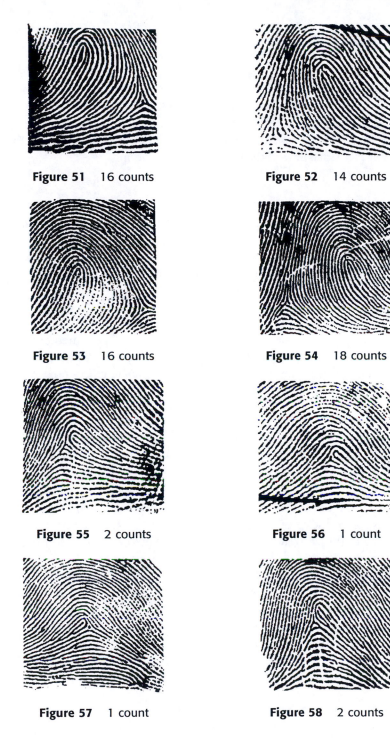

Figure 51   16 counts

Figure 52   14 counts

Figure 53   16 counts

Figure 54   18 counts

Figure 55   2 counts

Figure 56   1 count

Figure 57   1 count

Figure 58   2 counts

Radial and Ulnar Loops

A loop that flows in the direction of the ulna bone (little finger) is called an ulnar loop. The ridges of an ulnar loop enter the pattern area from the side nearest the little finger, curve at the top and end on the same side.

A radial loop is one that flows in the direction of the radius bone (thumb). The ridges of a radial loop enter the pattern area from the side nearest the thumb, curve at the top and end on the same side.

For purposes of testing, place the fingers of the hand just beneath the corresponding prints on the fingerprint card. Notice the direction of the type lines, if the type lines are diverging towards the little finger, the pattern is an ulnar loop and divergence toward the thumb is a radial loop.

PLAIN ARCH

In plain arches the ridges enter on one side of the fingerprint and flow or tend to flow out the other with a rise or wave in the center. The plain arch is very easily interpreted. There may be various ridge formations such as bifurcations, ending ridges, dots and islands in the plain arch, but the general ridge outline is the entering on one side, rising in the center and flowing out the opposite side. See Figures 59 to 70.

Tented Arches

There are three types of tented arches - angular, upthrust and loop type tented arch: Angular or angle type tented arch –*the type in which ridges at the center form a definite angle 90 degrees or less.* When ridges come in from opposite directions and meet in the center of the pattern an angle type tented arch is formed (Figures 71 to 73).

Upthrust tented arch– the type in which one or more ridges at the center form an upthrust. An upthrust is an ending ridge of any length rising from the horizontal plane; i.e., 45 degrees or more. The upthrust comes up from the bottom of the print where the ridges flow horizontally. There must be a space between it and the ridge immediately below it. An upthrust should not be confused with ending ridges, even though they end in the same abrupt manner. Upthrusts are slightly curved ridges that end upward and are not connected to any other ridge at the top or immediately below it. Figures 74 to 77 are examples of upthrust tented arches. Notice how the ridges in the center of the patterns form a peak. In Figure 76 three upthrusts can be clearly seen. No specific number is needed; if there is only one upthrust in the center, the pattern should be evaluated for an upthrust tented arch.

Loop type tented arch– the type in which a pattern has two of the basic requirements of the loop but does not have the third. At first glance, the loop type tented arch resembles a loop, but on closer examination does not have all the essential requirements for a loop: a sufficient recurve, a delta and a ridge count across a looping ridge. If the imaginary line drawn between delta and core does not cross a recurve (looping ridge), the pattern must be called a loop type tented arch. (See Examples in Figures 78 to 81.)

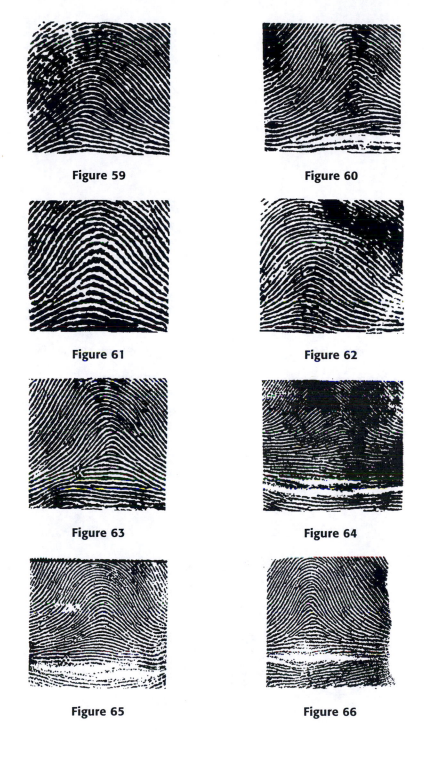

Figure 59

Figure 60

Figure 61

Figure 62

Figure 63

Figure 64

Figure 65

Figure 66

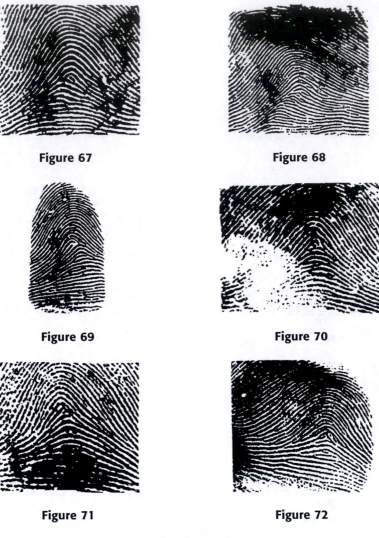

Figure 67

Figure 68

Figure 69

Figure 70

Figure 71

Figure 72

Figure 73

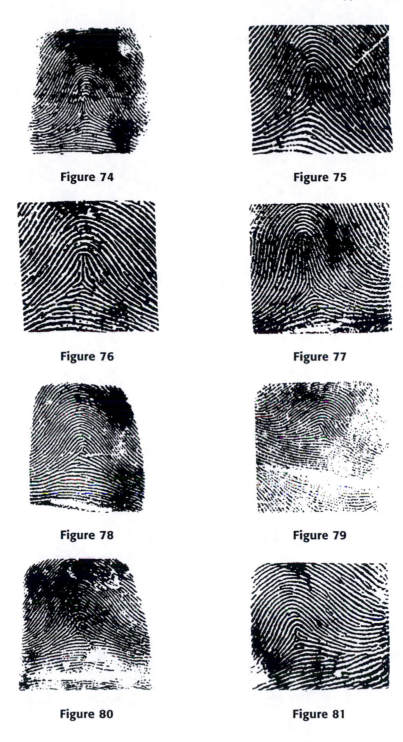

Figure 74

Figure 75

Figure 76

Figure 77

Figure 78

Figure 79

Figure 80

Figure 81

THE WHORL

The whorl is that type of pattern in which at least two deltas are present with a recurve in front of each delta.

The whorl pattern is divided into four divisions: plain, central pocket loop whorl, double loop whorl and accidental whorl. The whorl can be described as a circular pattern. When the ridges of a pattern flow in any form of a circle, it should be evaluated to determine if it is a whorl.

Plain Whorl

The plain whorl has three requirements:

1. Two deltas
2. A complete circuit (at least one, usually many)
3. An imaginary line between the two deltas must touch or cross at least one of the recurving ridges within the inner pattern area.

The complete circuit in a whorl may be spiral, circular, oval or any form of a circle. An appendage in the line of flow will spoil the recurve in front of a delta. A whorl must have a smooth recurve in front of each delta. Figures 82 to 96 are examples of plain whorls.

Figure 82

Figure 83

Figure 84

Figure 85

Figure 86

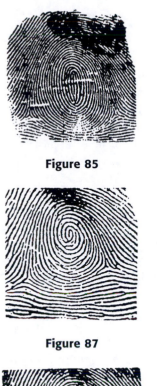

Figure 87

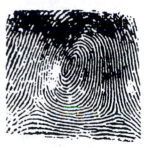

Figure 88

Figure 89

Figure 90

Figure 91

Figure 92

Central Pocket Loop Whorl

The central pocket loop whorl definition is similar to the plain whorl, the one exception is: *a line drawn between the two deltas does not touch or cross any recurring ridge within the inner pattern area.* Figures 97 to 108 are central pocket loop whorls. A recurving ridge which has an obstruction connected with it at a right angle to the inner line of flow will take the place of a free recurve and the pattern is still considered a central pocket loop. An obstruction may be described as a ridge that interrupts the imaginary line before it actually reaches the inner pattern area. See Figures 109 and 110. An obstruction may be either curved or straight.

The inner line of flow is determined by drawing an imaginary line between the inner delta and the center of the innermost recurve.

Double Loop Whorl

The double loop whorl *consists of two separate loop formations, with two separate and distinct sets of shoulders, and two deltas.* Figures 111 to120 are double loop whorls. The two loops of this type whorl must not be joined together by a common ridge as seen in Figure 121. No ridge count is needed for loops in a double loop whorl. The appendage rule is the same as that for plain loops. Figure122 is a plain loop. It is not a double loop because there are spoiled recurves on the right.

Accidental Whorl

The accidental whorl *is a pattern consisting of a combination of two different types of patterns, with the exception of the plain arch, with two or more deltas; or a pattern that conforms to none of the definitions.* It may be a combination of a loop and whorl, loop and tented arch, loop and central pocket loop, double loop and central pocket loop, or other combinations. The combination of loop and tented arch must have the loop formation over the tented arch (Figures 123-124-125). A formation where the tented arch appears over the loop is classified as a loop. See Figure 126.

Figures 123 to 125 are accidentals with a loop and tented arch. Figures 127 to 131 combine a loop and plain whorl or a central pocket loop. Figure 132 combines a loop and a double loop. Figure 133 combines a loop and plain arch and is classified as a loop. Figure 134 combines a loop and tented arch.

Whorl Tracing

The procedure for whorl tracing begins with locating the deltas. The ridge starting from the lower side or point of the extreme left delta is traced until the point opposite (or parallel to) the extreme right delta is reached. If the ridge traced passes above the right delta, and three or more ridges are between the tracing ridge and the delta, the tracing is designated as an "inner" –I (Figure 135). If the ridge traced passes below the right delta and three or more ridges are between the tracing ridge and delta, the tracing is an "outer" – O (Figure 136). All other tracings where less than 3 ridges are between the tracing ridge and delta designated as "meeting" –M (Figure 137 to 142). The symbols are listed below:

3 or more above the right delta = I

3 or more below the right delta = O

less than 3 in either direction = M

Tracing begins from the left delta. If the delta ends or is a dot, tracing is continued on the next lower ridge. A type line should never be used to begin tracing. In Figure 143 the typeline is used because it is the next lower ridge. When a ridge that is being traced ends abruptly, the tracing continues to the point on the next lower ridge immediately below where the ridge above ends. An example of this is shown in Figure 144. Short breaks in lines

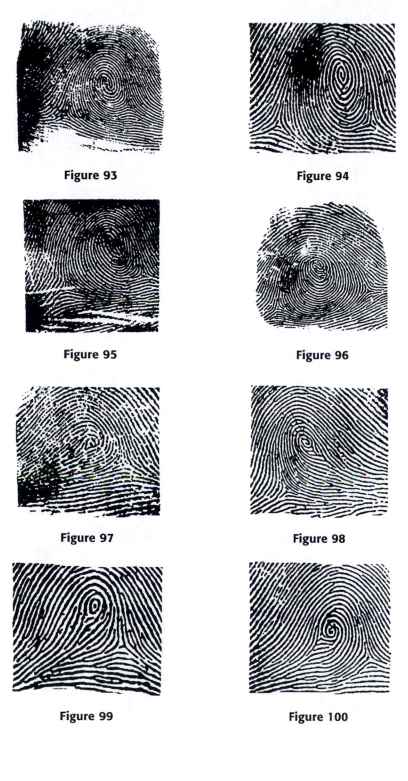

Figure 93

Figure 94

Figure 95

Figure 96

Figure 97

Figure 98

Figure 99

Figure 100

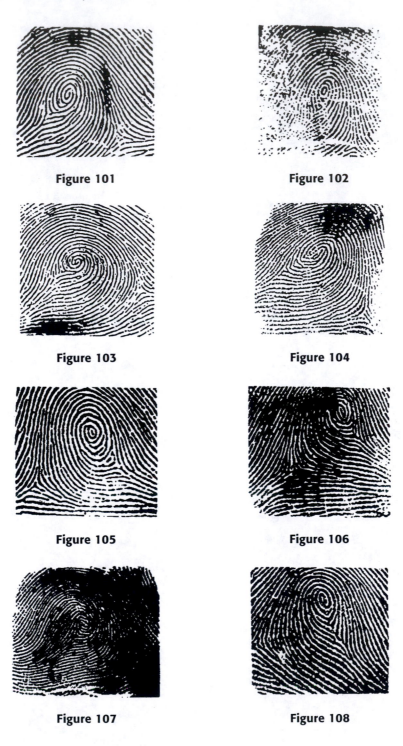

Figure 101

Figure 102

Figure 103

Figure 104

Figure 105

Figure 106

Figure 107

Figure 108

Figure 109

Figure 110

Figure 111

Figure 112

Figure 113

Figure 114

Figure 115

Figure 116

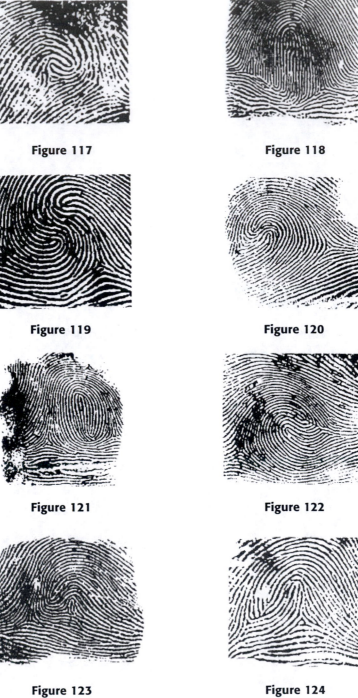

Figure 117

Figure 118

Figure 119

Figure 120

Figure 121

Figure 122

Figure 123

Figure 124

Figure 125

Figure 126

Figure 127

Figure 128

Figure 129

Figure 130

Figure 131

Figure 132

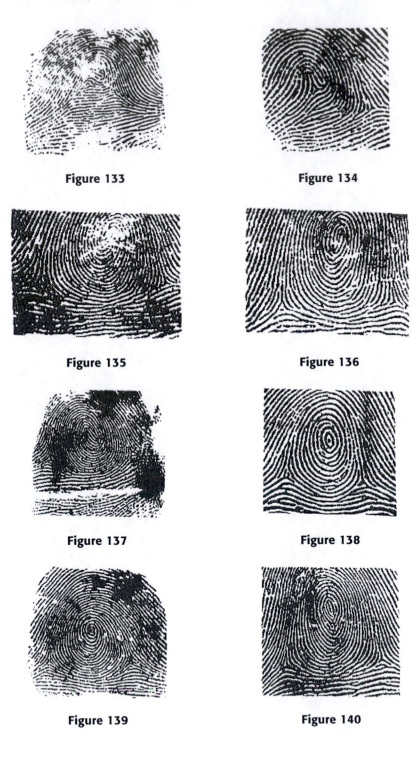

Figure 133

Figure 134

Figure 135

Figure 136

Figure 137

Figure 138

Figure 139

Figure 140

Figure 141

Figure 142

Figure 143

Figure 144

Figure 145

are sometimes due to improper inking, the presence of a foreign substance on the ridges, enlarged pores, disease or worn ridges. These are not considered to be definite ridge endings. The classifier will determine if a definite ending exists, and appropriate reference tracing should be done in all such cases. If the ridge traced bifurcates, follow the lowest branch. (See Figure 145.) Accidental whorls sometimes have three or more deltas. Only the extreme deltas are considered in tracing them. The tracing begins at the extreme left and continues to the extreme right delta as seen in Figure 146.

In a double loop or accidental whorl the rule of tracing is, *when the tracing passes inside of the right delta, stop at the nearest point to the right delta on the upward trend* (Figure 147). If there is no upward trend, the tracing continues until a point opposite the right delta or until the delta itself is reached (Figures 148 and 149).

Figure 146

Figure 147

Figure 148

Figure 149

CHAPTER III

Questionable Patterns

Patterns that are questionable are those that seem to have characteristics of two or more types of patterns. They can be classified by applying the exact definitions in choosing a preference.

Figure 150 has two loop formations. The one on the left has an appendage touching upon the shoulders of its recurve and is therefore a tented arch. The right portion of the fingerprint has all of the requirements of a loop. This pattern has two different types of patterns within it and would be classified as an accidental whorl except for the fact that it has only one delta. In order to be a whorl there must be at least two deltas present. In choosing between a tented arch and a loop, preference is given to the loop classification and this impression would be classified as a loop.

Figure 151 appears to be a whorl but on closer examination the part of the circuit in front of the right delta has an appendage touching it in the line of flow. This pattern is a one count loop.

Figure 152 is a plain arch. The dot in the center is not extended enough to be considered an upthrust. Dots are only considered in ridge counting or assigning a delta and must be as thick and heavy as the surrounding ridges. Figure 153 is similar to the previous illustration and is classified as a plain arch rather than a tented arch with a delta formation and two ending ridges.

Figure 154 has an appendage on each recurve on the left side and is classified as a central pocket loop whorl. In order to spoil the recurve of a whorl the appendage must be connected to the recurve at the point of contact with the line of flow.

In Figure 155 the impression has two good loop formations. It cannot be classified as a double loop whorl as it has only one delta. The classification of loop would not apply here since it would be difficult to make a choice between the two looping ridges. It is arbitrarily given the classification of a tented arch.

Figure 156 at first glance appears to be a loop but closer examination will show that one of the requirements of the loop is missing, i.e. a ridge count across a looping ridge. The core in this example is placed where the appendage of the innermost loop touches the next ridge that is the good recurve. If an imaginary line were placed between the delta and core, there would be no intervening ridges and therefore no ridge count. The pattern is classified as a tented arch.

Figure 157 is a pattern that has a delta and recurve with no ridge count across a looping ridge and is classified as a tented arch . The imaginary line between delta and core runs directly along the ridge, which is joined onto the side of the recurving ridge. Therefore, no ridge count is possible.

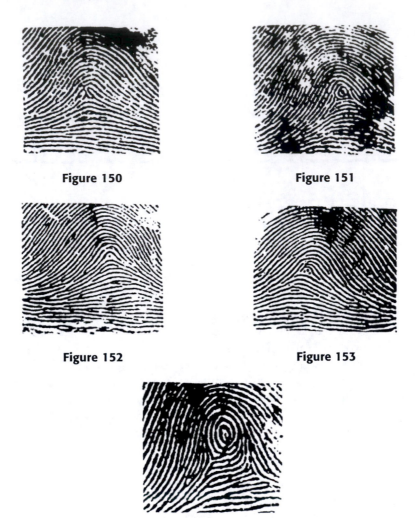

Figure 150

Figure 151

Figure 152

Figure 153

Figure 154

In Figure 158 there are three loop formations, each one is spoiled by an appendage touching upon its recurve between the shoulders at a right angle. It cannot be classified as an accidental whorl as the patterns are all of the same type. An accidental whorl is a combination of two or more different types of patterns excluding the plain arch. It is classified as a tented arch. Figure 159 consists of a loop over a dot with a second delta. The dot is not extended vertically and cannot be considered an upthrust. This pattern must be classified as a loop.

In Figure 160 the looping ridge A has an appendage abutting (touching) upon its recurve at a right angle and the recurve becomes spoiled as a result. The pattern is classified as a tented arch.

Figure 161 is a tented arch, which at first glance appears to be a whorl. It cannot be considered a whorl as the recurve on the left is spoiled by an appendage. The pattern is a tented arch of the type possessing two of the basic requirements of the loop but lacking the third. The delta and the sufficient recurve are present but the ridge count is missing.

Figure 155

Figure 156

Figure 157

Figure 158

Figure 159

Figure 160

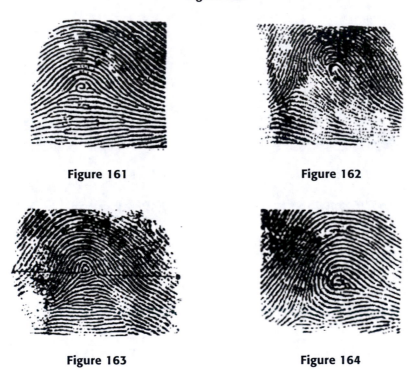

Figure 161

Figure 162

Figure 163

Figure 164

Figure 162 has two looping formations that would indicate a double loop whorl. However, the inner delta formation is located on the upper loop formation and this recurving ridge is eliminated from consideration. The pattern is classified as a loop.

Figure 163 is a loop with two counts; the delta is at B. There is a ridge making a complete circuit but point A cannot be used as a delta because it meets the definition of a type line. If the delta were placed on the recurve, the recurve would be spoiled.

Figure 164 is a loop pattern. The dots are not considered as obstructions crossing the line of flow at right angles. This rules out the classification of a central pocket loop whorl.

Figure 165 is a loop. Even though the pattern has two deltas, it cannot be called a whorl as the two recurving ridges have appendages and are considered spoiled.

Figure 166 is a tented arch. When analyzed closely an appendage will be seen between the shoulders of each possible recurve. No sufficient recurve is present.

Figure 165

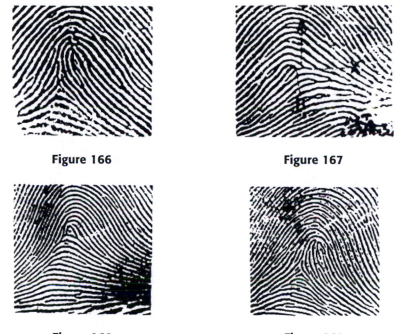

Figure 166   **Figure 167**

Figure 168   **Figure 169**

Figure 167 is classified as a plain arch. There is no angle in the center. The ridges seen outlined in the center are bifurcations rather than two ridges touching at an angle.

Figure 168 is a tented arch because of the angle made when the curving ridge above the dot touches upon the ridge directly under and to the left of the dot.

Figure 169 is a loop. The pattern has two separate looping ridge formations next to each other upon the same side of a common delta. It is not a double loop whorl as there is only one delta formation. In locating the core, the two looping ridges are treated as one loop with two rods in the center. The core is on the left shoulder of the far loop and there is a ridge count of four.

CHAPTER IV

The Classification Formula

The first step in classifying prints is to interpret each pattern beginning with the right thumb and place the pattern type or symbol in the lower right hand corner of the fingerprint card. Ridge counts of loops and whorl tracings are shown in the upper right hand corner. This procedure is called *blocking out.* Ulnar loops in any finger are shown by a diagonal line slanting in the direction of the loop. In the formula a capital "U" is used. Whorls are shown as the letter "w." Plain arches as "a," tented arches as "t," and radial loops as "r." The right hand classification is placed above the left hand on the line provided for the formula. All references are placed in the space provided.

The following paragraphs will discuss every division of the Henry classification formula :

Key: The key is obtained by counting the ridges of the first loop on the fingerprint card with the exception of the little finger. It is the first division of the classification and is placed on the top line.

Major division: The major division is placed just to the right of the key in the classification formula. It is obtained by determining the tracing or ridge count of left and right thumb. When loops appear, a table is used to convert the ridge counts into the small, medium, or large groups and are shown by the letters S, M, L. If loops appear in both thumbs, the left thumb is determined first. (See the *Classification Chart.*) Classifying the left thumb first will determine which chart should be used for the right. No conversion is needed for whorls. The tracings I, M , or O are used.

Primary: The primary classification is the numerical value of whorls on a fingerprint card. Each square is assigned a value. Only whorls are considered in determining the primary. Squares 1 and 2 are given the value of 16. Squares 3 and 4 have a value of 8. Squares 5 and 6 have a value of 4. Squares 7 and 8 have the value of 2 and Squares 9 and 10 have the value of 1. The guidelines for *assigning the primary* show the numerical value assigned to each square.

The even number squares containing whorls are totaled and 1 is added to the result. The odd number squares containing whorls are totaled and 1 is added to the result. The plus 1 is called the *arbitrary one.* The primary is written as a fraction with even number squares +1 over odd number squares +1. If no whorls are present in a set of fingerprints, the primary 1 over 1 is used. If there are no whorls in the even number squares and the odd number squares have whorls, the primary for the even number squares is 1. Also, if there are no whorls in the odd number squares. the primary for the odd number squares is 1. The primary is placed to the right of the major.

Secondary: *The secondary is the pattern type of the index fingers written in capital letters.* The secondary is placed to the right of the primary. Only the first letter of the pattern is shown using the letters A, T, R, U, W.

Sub-Secondary: The sub-secondary is obtained from the Index, Middle, and Ring fingers. The ridge counts of loops are converted into either I or O. Whorl tracings *I, M, O* are placed in the formula as they appear. (See *Classification Chart*.) The sub-secondary is placed immediately to the right of the secondary and is written in capital letters.

Final: The final is determined by the ridge count of the right little finger and is placed to the right of the sub-secondary. If a loop does not appear in the right little finger, a loop in the left little is used. If no loops appear in the little fingers a whorl may be used to obtain a final, counting from left delta to core if in the right hand and from right delta to core in the left hand.

Pattern codes for blocking out a fingerprint card

Arch . . . . a

Tented Arch . . . . . . t

Radial Loop . . . . . . r

Ulnar Loop . . . . . . \ (right hand)
/ (left hand)

The ulnar is brought up in the formula as U

Whorl . . . . w

The appropriate capital letters are used for the Index fingers.

CHAPTER V

Classification Chart

9	M O	29 18	W R	OIM OII	10
Key	**Major**	**Primary**	**Secondary**	**Sub-Secondary**	**Final**
Ridge count of first loop except little finger	Both thumbs, convert ridge counts to S, M, L. Determine left thumb first. Use whorl tracings for whorls	Numerical value of whorls even+1 odd+1	First letter of pattern type in index fingers; ATRUW, use capital letters	Index, middle, ring fingers; convert ridge counts to I or O; use whorl tracings for whorls	Ridge count of little finger

RIGHT HAND

R. Thumb	R. Index	R. Middle	R. Ring	R. Little
CHART A When left thumb is 16 or less 1 – 11 = S 12 – 16 = M 17 and over = L **CHART B** When left thumb is 17 or over 1 – 17 = S 18 – 22 = M 23 and over = L	1 – 9 = I 10 and over = O	1 – 10 = I 11 and over = O	1 – 13 = I 14 and over = O	

LEFT HAND

L. Thumb	L. Index	L. Middle	L. Ring	L. Little
1 – 11 = S 12 – 16 = M 17 and over = L	VALUES	SAME	AS	ABOVE

ASSIGNING THE PRIMARY
NUMERICAL VALUE OF WHORLS FOR PRIMARY

Even+1

Odd+1

16	16	8	8	4
1. R.Thumb	2. R. Index	3. R. Middle	4. R. Ring	5. R. Little
4	2	2	1	1
6. L. Thumb	7. L. Index	8. L. Middle	9. L. Ring	10. L. Little

CHAPTER VI

Small Letter Classification

Small letters are *arches, tented arches, and radial loops in any finger except the index fingers.* As mentioned earlier, patterns in the index fingers are shown as capital. All others are written as small letters (lower case). The presence of any small letter on the fingerprint card will be classified using the small letter classification rules listed below. At first small letters may seem confusing but in a short time it will be realized that they are very easy. The sub-secondary in a small letter classification will differ from the usual sub-secondary. It will include the secondary and a grouping of all small letters.

The classifier should block out the card as usual, then proceed to do ridge counts and or whorl tracings. After the card is blocked out the procedure for classifying may differ according to the position of the small letters. After the *secondary* is assigned, a good rule to follow is to review every finger block beginning with the thumb and show small letters in the exact position as they appear. (See Small Letter Classification Example.) Never show the index finger pattern as a small letter, even if it is A, T, or R. It is not considered a division of the small letter classification formula.

SMALL LETTER RULES

1. If either or both thumbs is an arch or tented arch, there is no major division. It is permissible to show the key in parenthesis.

2. Small letter thumbs will appear in the formula between the primary and secondary.

3. Never show another pattern between the secondary and a small letter.

4. A dash is used for a pattern not shown.

SMALL LETTER CLASSIFICATION EXAMPLES

(12)   1aT _ _ t

　　　1 Aa   5

		12	3	
a	T	\	\	t
15			7	5
/	A	a	/	/

13 O 5 Uatr 11

　　I 17 Ua

O	13			11
w	/	a	t	r
I	5		8	2
w	/	a	/	/

EXTENSIONS

The Second subsecondary classification: The second subsecondary is an excellent way to make a very large file easier to search when the filing system consists of the Henry formula. It is used in those sections of the file where the subsecondary is a combination of all inners or outers. The symbols S, M, L are used and are brought up in the formula directly above the subsecondary, the right hand being the numerator and the left hand the denominator. The following table is used:

1 to 05 inclusive, S	01 to 08 inclusive, S	01 to 10 inclusive, S
06 to 12 inclusive, M	09 to 14 inclusive, M	11 to 18 inclusive, M
13 or more, L	15 or more, L	19 or more, L

WHORL EXTENSIONS

In the extensions used for large whorl groups, the type of whorl is shown by the symbols W, C, D, or X for the index fingers and w, c, d, x for all other fingers. The breakdown of the symbols are: W (plain whorl), C (central pocket loop whorl), D (double loop whorl), and X (accidental whorl). These symbols are used for subclassification purposes only and are brought up into the formula directly above the subsecondary in their respective positions.

SPECIAL LOOP EXTENSIONS

The ridge counts in fingers Nos. 2, 3, 4, 7, 8, 9 and in certain instances, No. 10 are used for the all loop group in the special loop extension. The number values are brought up in the classification formula directly above the subsecondary. When there are all loops the following special loop extensions may be used:

1 – 4 1	9 – 12 3	17 – 20 5	25 and over 7
5 – 8 2	13 – 16 4	21 – 24 6	

REFERENCING

Emphasis should be placed on the necessity of referencing questionable patterns whether it be in the ridge count, the tracing or the pattern type. There are many reasons for referencing: variation in individual judgment and eyesight, worn ridges due to age or occupations, temporary and permanent scars, crippled hands, bandaged fingers and amputations. If the prints are inked impressions, the amount of ink and pressure used in taking the prints may make it necessary to reference.

In the Henry formula, when a ridge count is obtained and is *borderline,* a reference should be made at all times. In the classification chart the ridge counts are translated into symbols, i.e.; (1 – 9 = I) (10 and over = O). An index finger with a 9 count would be given a reference of 10. If the ridge count is 10, a reference of 9 is given. This procedure should be followed whenever ridge counts on any finger are *borderline* according to the *Classification Chart.*

If there is doubt as to which classification should be assigned to a pattern, it is given the preferred classification and reference searches are conducted in all other possible classifications.

On the fingerprint card a line is provided for the classification formula and an additional line for references. For example:

$$\text{Class} \quad \frac{22 \text{ M } 1\text{U} \quad \text{III} \quad 19}{\text{L} \quad 1\text{U} \quad \text{OII}}$$

$$\text{Ref} \quad \frac{22 \text{ M } 1\text{R} \quad \text{III} \quad 19}{\text{L} \quad 1\text{U} \quad \text{OII}} \quad \text{(The Right index finger has been referenced to "R")}$$

CHAPTER VII

Classification of Amputations—Missing at Birth—Scarred Patterns

When one or more amputations appear upon a fingerprint card it should be noted on the fingerprint card indicating that a certain finger or fingers have been amputated or missing at birth. If one finger is amputated, it is classified as the same pattern in the opposite finger including ridge count or tracing and referenced to every other possible classification.

If two or more fingers are amputated, they are given classifications identical with the fingers opposite, with no other reference.

If two amputated fingers are opposite each other, both are given the classification of whorls with meet tracings.

If all 10 fingers are amputated or missing at birth, the classification will be:

$$\frac{\text{M 32 W MMM}}{\text{M 32 W MMM}}$$

CLASSIFICATION OF SCARRED PATTERNS

When a fingerprint is so scarred and the pattern type cannot be determined, the impression is given the classification of the corresponding finger on the other hand. If the pattern is partially scarred and the pattern type can be determined, the impression should be given the subclassification as indicated by the ridges.

When there is a scarred pattern, both sides of the scar should be examined closely to try and determine the continuation of the severed ridges. In some instances, accurate tracings or ridge counts are made by using great care.

If fingers are injured to the extent it is impossible to secure impressions, the unprinted fingers are given classifications identical with the opposite finger.

CHAPTER VIII

The National Crime Information Center (NCIC)

The National Crime Information Center (NCIC) is a computerized information center established for all law enforcement agencies local, state, and federal. The system is located at FBI Headquarters in Washington, D.C. and stores huge amounts of information on individuals whom warrants are outstanding or who have committed an offense that is classified as a felony or serious misdemeanor. Parole and probation violators are included in the files.

Specific codes are used for the NCIC Fingerprint Classification (FPC). A 20 block character field is used. Two letters are to be used for each finger as shown on the next page.

Pattern Type	Pattern Subgroup	NCIC FPC Code
ARCH	Plain Arch	AA
	Tented Arch	TT
LOOP	Radial Loop	2 numeric characters. Determine ridge count and add fifty (50). If the count is 16, add 50 for a sum of 66.
	Ulnar Loop	2 numeric characters indicating the actual ridge count (less than 50). If the count is less than 10, precede by zero. e.g., ridge count of 14, enter as 14; ridge count of 9, enter as 09.
WHORL	Plain Whorl	Enter "P" followed by whorl tracing.
	Inner Tracing	PI
	Meeting Tracing	PM
	Outer Tracing	PO
	Central Pocket Loop Whorl	Enter "C" followed by whorl tracing
		CI
		CM
		CO
	Double Loop Whorl	Enter "d" followed by whorl pattern Notice the small letter "d" is used.
	Inner Tracing	dI
	Meeting Tracing	dM
	Outer Tracing	dO
WHORL	Accidental Whorl	Enter "X" followed by
	Inner Whorl	whorl tracing
		XI
		XM
		XO
MISSING/AMPUTATED FINGER		XX
COMPLETELY SCARRED OR MUTILATED PATTERN		SR

The NCIC codes are written in the small blocks that appear just below the classification and reference lines. An example of the NCIC FPC for a set of fingerprints made up of all ulnar loops would read:

1	8	1	5	1	2	1	0	1	3	0	6	0	8	1	2	0	3	2	1

The same set of fingerprints with #2 and #7 as radial loops would be as follows:

1	8	6	5	1	2	1	0	1	3	0	6	5	8	1	2	0	3	2	1

CHAPTER IX

Procedures for Processing Fingerprints

HOW TO TAKE INKED FINGERPRINTS

The basic equipment needed for taking fingerprints are an inking plate, a cardholder, printer's ink, and a roller. In order to get clear, distinct fingerprints, it is necessary to spread the ink in a thin, even coating on a small inking plate. A roller is best for use as a spreader. The size used is determined by individual needs and preferences. A roller 3- by 1-inch is satisfactory.

An inking plate is usually made from a hard, scratch resistant metal plate 6 inches wide by 14 inches long or by inlaying a block of wood with a piece of glass one-fourth of an inch thick, 6 inches wide, and 14 inches long. If the glass is used by itself, it should be fixed to a base in order to prevent breakage. The inking surface should be high enough to allow the subject's forearm to be in a horizontal position when the fingers are being inked. The plate may be placed in such a position that the operator can avoid unnecessary pressure or accidental strain and obtain more even impressions. The fingerprints should be taken on an 8- by 8-inch card.

There are two types of impressions that are involved in the process of taking fingerprints. The upper 10 prints are taken individually, thumb, index, middle, ring, and little fingers of each hand. These fingers are rolled from side to side and should be rolled in the order named. All available ridge detail should be obtained. They are called "rolled" impressions. At the bottom of the card smaller impressions of the fingers of each hand are taken at the same time without rolling.

The "plain" or "simultaneous" impressions are used to check on the sequence and accuracy of the rolled impressions. It is better to ink and print each finger separately. When preparing to take a set of fingerprints, a small amount of ink is placed on the inking glass or slab and rolled thoroughly until a thin, even film covers the surface.

The subject should stand in front of and at forearm's length from the inking plate. In taking the rolled impressions the side of the bulb of the finger is placed on the inking plate and the finger is rolled to the other side until it faces the opposite direction. The finger to be printed is inked evenly from the tip to the below the first joint. The operator should press the finger lightly on the card and a clear rolled impression of the finger surface will be obtained. The thumbs are rolled toward and the fingers away from the center of the subject's body. An effective way to help the subject relax while the fingerprints are being taken is to tell him/her to look at some far-away object and not to look at his/her hands.

In order to obtain "plain" impressions, all the fingers of the right hand should be pressed lightly on the inking plate, then pressed all together upon the lower right hand corner of the card in the space provided.

LIVE SCAN

Live Scan is a new addition to the method of taking fingerprints. This is a way of getting fingerprints into the system without the need for taking inked impressions. A Live Scan fingerprint console contains a fingerprint scanner, printer and software needed to enter the fingerprints directly into an automated system. An applicant or arrested person's fingers are rolled on a glass platen with a scanner below the glass. The scanner provides an image of the print on a monitor at the console. The operator can examine the fingerprint. If the scan is not good, the operator can erase and recapture the print. When all prints are acceptable, the prints may be searched against the inked fingerprint database of millions of persons to determine the identity of the person. If the person's fingerprints have been previously entered into the system, a fingerprint examiner can verify the person's identity with the older print.

FINGERPRINT COMPARISON

In the comparison of fingerprints, the examiner should take into consideration: *identical pattern type, quality and quantity of ridge characteristics that are alike, likeness of location of ridge characteristics.*

The Ridge characteristics must match in each fingerprint. Although there are no laws in the United States regarding the number of matching ridge characteristics before an identity is established, the examiner must be absolutely certain of his findings and conclusions before the evidence is introduced in a court of law.

The direction and position of each characteristic will determine whether or not the fingerprints being compared were made by the same person. The examiner should ask himself: how many ridge counts are there to the left or right of another ridge ending, bifurcation, or any other distinctive characteristic? Is a ridge or bifurcation pointing up, down, right or left? The fingerprint examiner who makes the identification should be convinced that the identification is correct. However, in all instances another person, usually a supervisor will also examine the fingerprint comparison before it is presented in court.

The final result of all the efforts of fingerprint examiners and the very reason for the existence of an Identification Section within any police department comes to its ultimate conclusion in a court of law.

FILING SEQUENCE FOR FINGERPRINTS

The following filing sequence should be followed for any file system that uses the Henry system of classification.

Primary:

$$\frac{1}{1} \text{ to } \frac{32}{32}$$

All prints with the primary 1 over 1 are filed together, followed by 2 over 1, 3 over 1, until 32 over 1 is reached. Then 1 over 2, 2 over 2, etc. until the 32 over 32 primary is reached.

An example of fingerprints to be filed would be arranged in this order:

1. Prints having the same primary
2. Pattern Type sequence using the examples below (ATRUW)
3. Sub-secondary arranged according to IMO classification
4. Final is placed in numerical order with prints having the same ridge count grouped together
5. The key is also sequenced by the ridge count

When small letters are present there are 25 possible combinations that can appear in the index fingers. They are as follows:

Secondary:

A T R U W	A T R U W	<u>A T R U W</u>	<u>A T R U W</u>	A T R U W
A A A A A	T T T T T	R R R R R	U U U U U	W W W W

Secondary loop and whorl group:

$$\frac{R}{R} \text{ to } \frac{W}{W}$$

There are nine possible combinations that can appear in the index fingers. They are:

$$\frac{R}{R} \quad \frac{U}{R} \quad \frac{W}{R}$$

$$\frac{R}{U} \quad \frac{U}{U} \quad \frac{W}{U}$$

$$\frac{R}{W} \quad \frac{U}{W} \quad \frac{W}{W}$$

Sub-Secondary

$$\frac{III}{III} \text{ to } \frac{OOO}{OOO}$$

Each group of the numerator becomes the denominator for the complete sequence of numerators listed below. The sequence of the sub-secondary is as follows:

$\frac{III}{III}$	$\frac{IIM}{III}$	$\frac{IIO}{III}$	$\frac{IMI}{III}$	$\frac{IMM}{III}$	$\frac{IMO}{III}$
$\frac{IOI}{III}$	$\frac{IOM}{III}$	$\frac{IOO}{III}$	$\frac{MII}{III}$	$\frac{MIM}{III}$	$\frac{MIO}{III}$
$\frac{MMI}{III}$	$\frac{MMM}{III}$	$\frac{MMO}{III}$	$\frac{MOI}{III}$	$\frac{MOM}{III}$	$\frac{MOO}{III}$
$\frac{OII}{III}$	$\frac{OIM}{III}$	$\frac{OIO}{III}$	$\frac{OMI}{III}$	$\frac{OMM}{III}$	$\frac{OMO}{III}$
$\frac{OOI}{III}$	$\frac{OOM}{III}$	$\frac{OOO}{III}$	etc. To	$\frac{OOO}{OOO}$	

Major:

The following sequence is used:

When loops appear in both thumbs the sequence is as follows:

$$\frac{\text{S M L S M L S M L}}{\text{S S S M M M L L L}}$$

When whorls appear in both thumbs the sequence is:

$$\frac{\text{I M O I M O I M O}}{\text{I I I M M M O O O}}$$

When a whorl appears in the right thumb and a loop in the left, the sequence is:

$$\frac{\text{I M O I M O I M O}}{\text{S S S M M M L L L}}$$

When a loop appears in the right thumb and a whorl in the left, the sequence is:

$$\frac{\text{S M L S M L S M L}}{\text{I I I M M M O O O}}$$

Final:

The final is filed in numerical sequence. If there are 12 prints having a final of 14 all of them should be filed together and followed by those prints in the same group having a final of 15.

Key:

The key is also filed in numerical sequence in the same way as the final.

Special Loop Extension has a sequence of:

$$\frac{111}{111} \text{ etc, to } \frac{777}{777}$$

Formula Sample

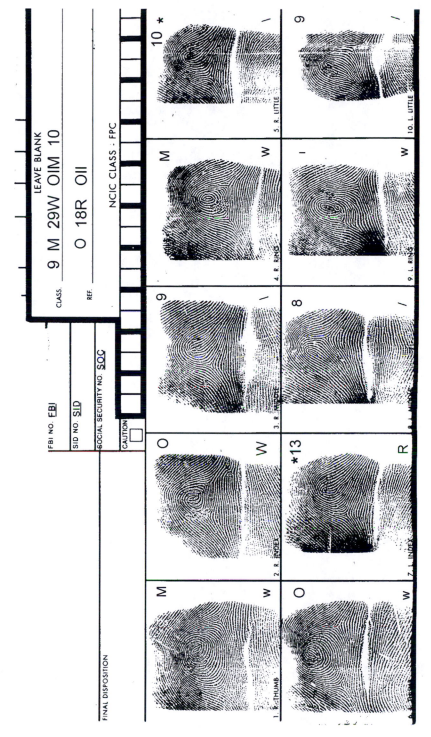

APPENDIX A

1. Missing Deltas

   When the delta is missing a delta has to be assigned. Look at the side of the fingerprint where the ridges are diverging. At the edge of the print where the delta should be, the ridges spread apart and go in opposite directions. In the center of these ridges you can place a dot for the delta. From this point draw an imaginary line to the core. If there are no diverging ridges visible, another procedure is to draw a diagonal line from the core to the area where the delta should be. A plus sign may be placed after the ridge count indicating there may be more ridges that are not seen. If no delta is seen on a whorl the same procedure is done with referencing to either I, M, or O.

2. Determining Ulnar and Radial Loops

   A looping ridge (recurve in a loop) has one side which is open. The recurve begins with a line that comes up from the bottom, curves at the top, continues downward and ends on the same side from which it entered. A good example is found on Page 9, Figure 23. The word "core" is pointing to the recurve. The open end is at the bottom of the recurve where the ridges end. In determining the pattern type it is necessary to decide if the opening is on the little finger side of the hand or the thumb side. Loops which are open on the little finger side of the hand are ulnar and loops with the open end on the thumb side are radial. Always look at the back of the hand when making the decision. For test purposes, place the fingers of the hand you are classifying underneath the corresponding prints appearing on a fingerprint card. If the ridges end on the little finger side, the pattern is an ulnar. If they end on the thumb side it is a radial. The same test applies to the left hand.

3. Henry Classification Formula

   Guidelines for Thumb Charts and All Whorl Classification. When classifying a fingerprint card for the Major and both thumbs are loops, classify the left thumb first. Classifying the left thumb first will determine which chart should be used for the right thumb. Chart A and B are shown under the right hand chart in the Classification Chart. The formula position for the left thumb in the Major is numerator and denominator for the right thumb. If the left thumb is a whorl and the right thumb is a loop, Chart A is used to determine the right thumb.

When all whorls are present on a fingerprint card, the Key and Final are obtained by counting the whorl in the right thumb and the little finger respectively. If in the right hand, a whorl is counted from left delta to core and from right delta to core in the left hand. The double loop whorl is counted from the delta to core of the upright loop. If there are two or more cores (usually applies to accidental whorls), the ridge count is made from left delta (right hand) or right delta (left hand) to the core which is the least number of ridges distant from the delta. The double loop is counted from the delta to the core of the upright loop. Where loops of a double loop are horizontal, the nearest core is chosen.

Simultaneous Impressions. Simultaneous impressions are found below the ten fingerprints on a card. If the classifier is in doubt concerning the sequence of the fingers in the squares, it is a simple matter to view the simultaneous impressions to see if the fingers are in the proper order. Many times these impressions are easier to analyze. The right thumb and right fingers are placed on the right side at the bottom of the fingerprint card and the left thumb and left fingers are placed on the left side.

4. Small Letter Classification

If there is an **a, t, r** in any finger block except the index (it should be capitalized), the formula for this is considered small letter classification. The best way to complete this type of classification is to begin with: (1)KEY (2) Major. If there is an a, or t in either thumb there is no Major because you cannot mix the small a's and t's with I, M, O, S, L used in the Major. (3) Figure the PRIMARY and (4) Complete the SECONDARY. After you have placed all these divisions on the fingerprint card, go back over the card starting with the thumb. Look at each block and if there is an a, t, or r in any finger (except Index), position them exactly in the formula as they appear on the fingerprint card. Never show a loop or whorl between the secondary and a small letter. A dash is shown instead.

Small letters are easy to classify when understood. Interpreting the patterns is the most challenging part of the procedure. When plain arch (A) or tented arch (T) patterns are in the index fingers they are not considered small letters. They are written as capitals and are not repeated in the subsecondary. In this instance, the subsecondary will not consist of three letters. There will only be two. Should both little fingers be an a or t, no final is used.

APPENDIX B

Page 133, Exercise 13 and 14

Page 139, Exercise 17

Page 141, Exercise 18

Complete the FBI NCIC codes for the above exercises
Subsecondary Exercise on Page 91, #1 left middle finger whorl is I

PART II

Fingerprint Classification Exercises

NAME THE MATCHING CHARACTERISTICS AND GIVE THE CORRECT DEFINITION

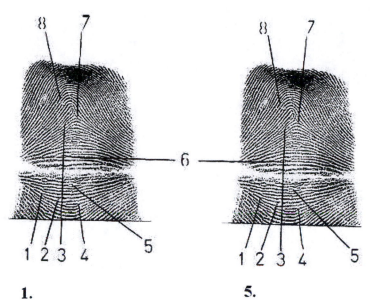

1.

2.

3.

4.

5.

6.

7.

8.

LOCATE EACH TYPELINE AND DRAW A LINE ON EACH ONE

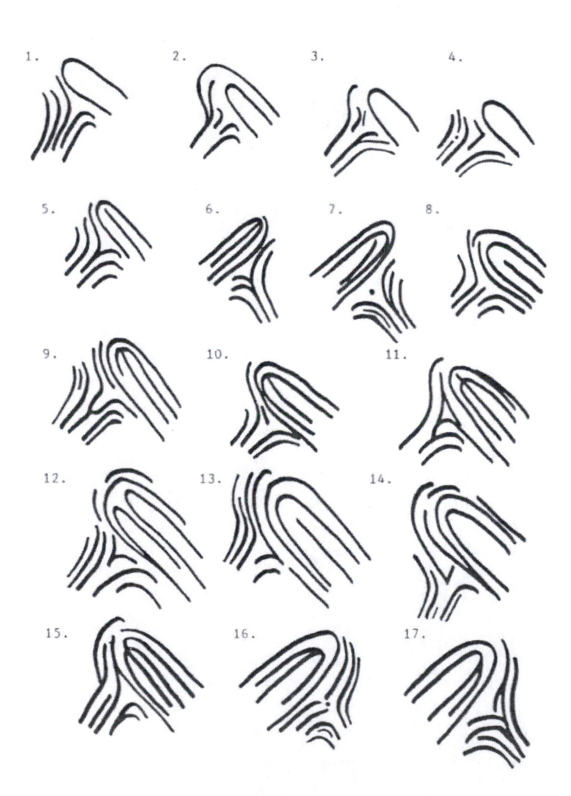

SHOW LOCATION OF DELTA AND CORE BY PLACING "D" AND "C" ON THE FOLLOWING

1.

2.

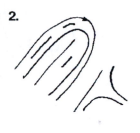

3.

4.

5.

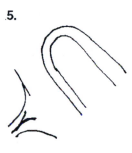

6.

7.

8.

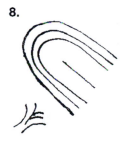

9.

10.

ASSIGN DELTA AND CORE

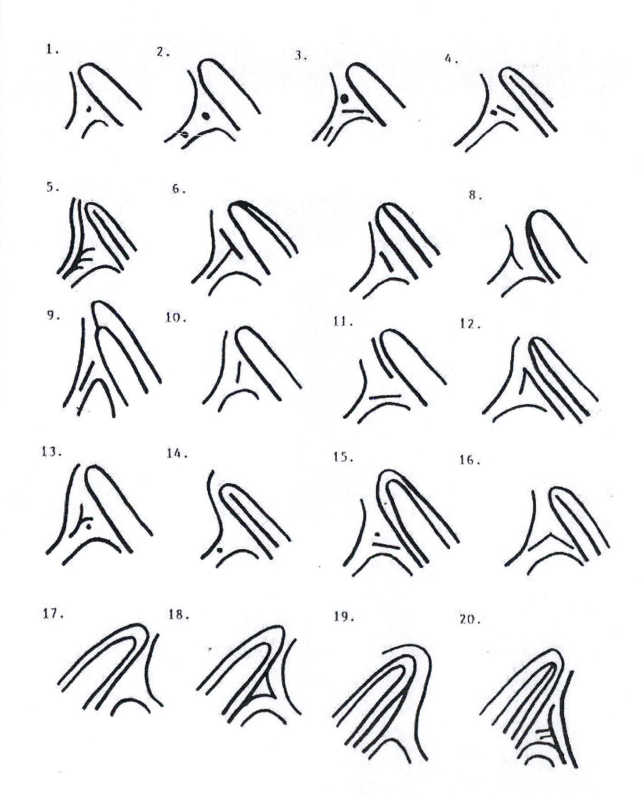

RIDGE COUNT ILLUSTRATION

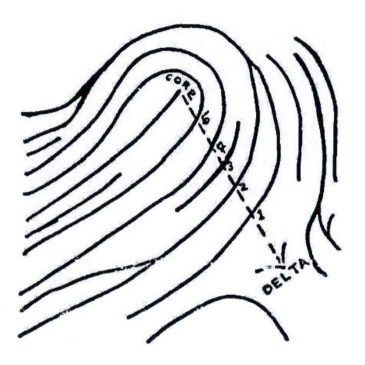

RIDGE COUNT PRACTICE EXERCISE 1

1
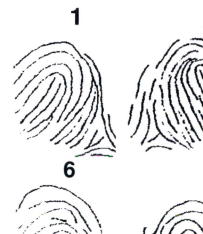

2

3

4

5

6

7

8

9

10

11

12

13

14

15

16

17

18

PLACE THE RIDGE COUNT UNDER EACH PATTERN

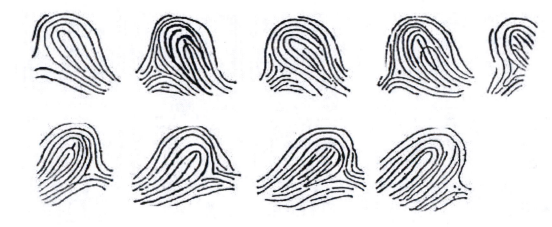

PLACE THE RIDGE COUNT BELOW EACH FINGERPRINT

ULNAR AND RADIAL LOOPS

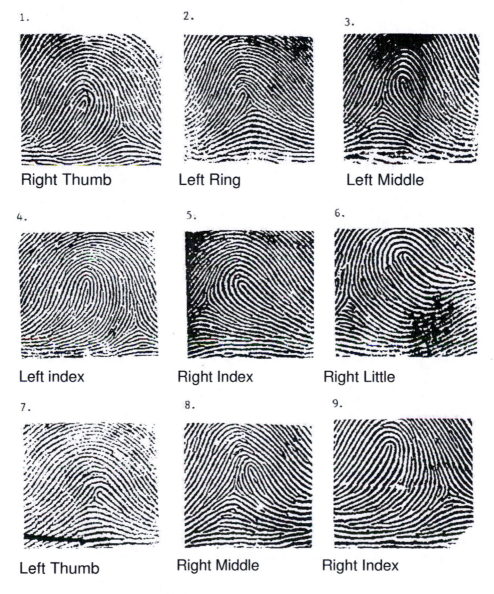

1.

Right Thumb

2.

Left Ring

3.

Left Middle

4.

Left index

5.

Right Index

6.

Right Little

7.

Left Thumb

8.

Right Middle

9.

Right Index

WRITE THE PATTERN TYPE NEXT TO NUMBERS SHOWN

LOOP-TYPE QUIZ

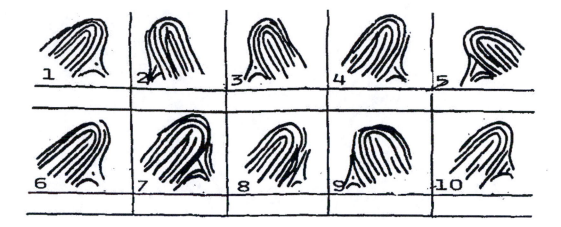

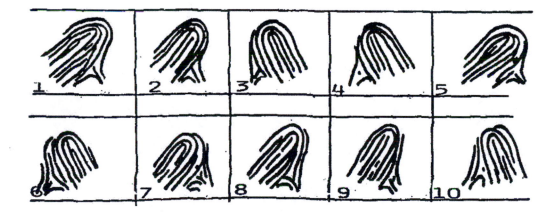

ARCHES AND TENTED ARCHES

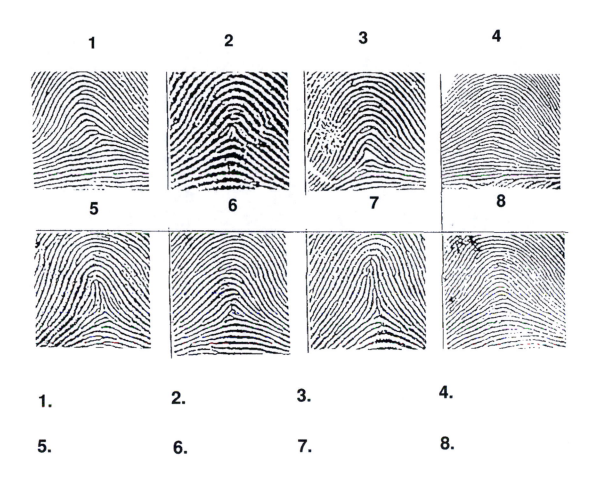

1.   2.   3.   4.

5.   6.   7.   8.

PATTERN RECOGNITION 1

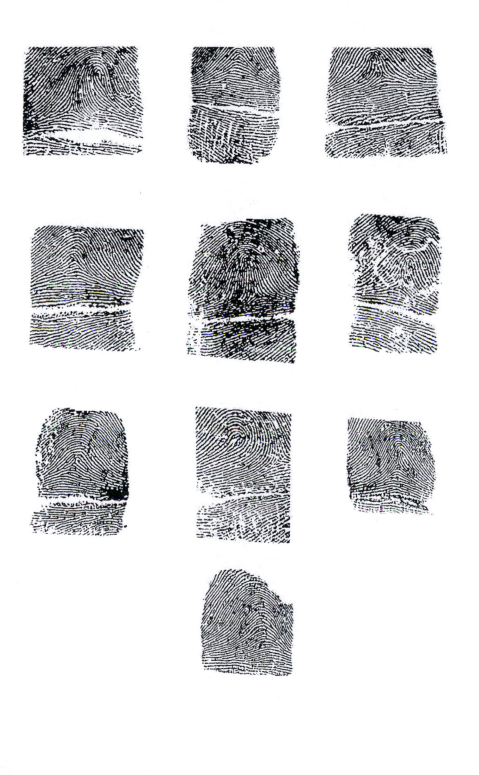

IDENTIFY EACH PATTERN

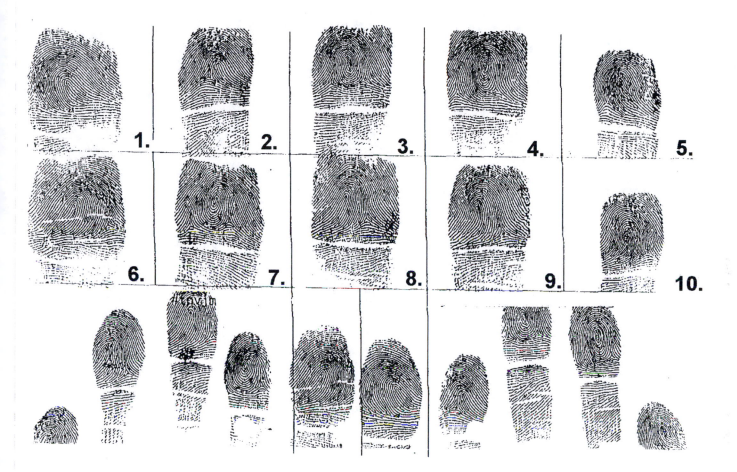

1.

2.

3.

4.

5.

6.

7.

8.

9.

10.

WHORL PRACTICE EXERCISE 1

How many lines are between the tracing line and the right delta?
What is the tracing called?

WHORL PRACTICE EXERCISE 2

How many lines are between the tracing line and the right delta?
What is the tracing called?

WHORL TRACING EXERCISE 1

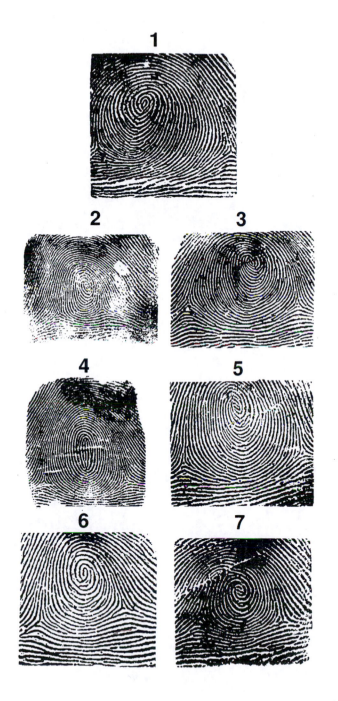

WHORL TRACING EXERCISE 2

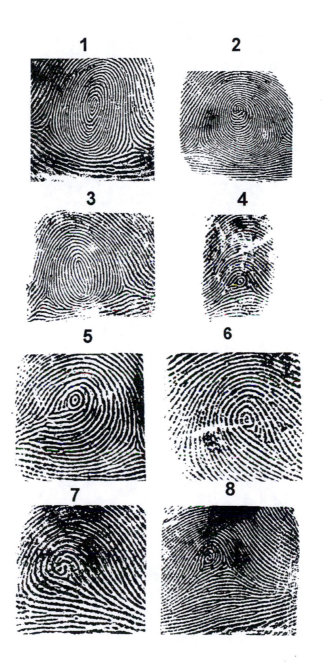

	RT	LT	DETERMINE MAJOR DIVISION	
1.	17	12		
2.	23	15		
3.	15	14		
4.	17	18		
5.	17	14		
6.	22	I		
7.	23	18		
8.	14	16		
9.	22	16		
10.	18	17		
11.	0	19		
12.	20	16		
13.	19	19		
14.	18	21		
15.	20	I		
16.	11	17		
17.	12	18		
18.	25	5		
19	22	13		
20	M	0		

What is the major in the following instances?

21. The left thumb ridge count is 5 and the right thumb is a plain arch.
22. A whorl tracing of M appears in both thumbs.
23. The right thumb is amputated and the left thumb has a 12 count loop.
24. Tented arches are in both thumbs.
25. There is a ridge count of 1 in the right thumb and 2 in the left thumb.

SUBSECONDARY EXERCISE

```
        O   O   11                          10   2   5
1.....U  W   W   U   U   =        8.....W   R    U   U   W   =
      W  U   W   U   U                 U   A    U   U   W
        11   3   15                         10   8


        M   I   8                           I    2   I
2.....U  W   W   W   U   =        9.....U   W    U   W   U   =
      U  U   W   W   U                 U   U    U   U   U
        8    M   M                         10    8   4


        12  15  19                          9    19
3.....U  R   U   U   U   =        10.....W  T    U   U   W   =
      U  U   U   U   U                  W   R    U   U   W
        8   11  18                          11   7   17


        5   9   I
4.....U  R   U   W   U   =
      U  W   W   U   W
        I   I   11


        O   13  11
5.....W  W   U   U   W   =
      U  U   W   W   U
        9   M   I


        18  I   13
6.....U  R   W   U   U   =
      U  A   U   W   U
            5   M


        I   I   I
7.....W  W   W   W   W   =
      U  R   U   U   W
        20  12  6
```

ASSIGN THE PRIMARY

1.

W 1.	2.	3.	W 4.	5.
W 6.	W 7.	8.	9.	W 10.

2.

1.	2.	3.	4.	W 5.
W 6.	7.	8.	W 9.	10.

3.

W 1.	2.	W 3.	4.	5.
6.	W 7.	8.	W 9.	10.

4.

W 1.	2.	3.	4.	5.
W 6.	7.	8.	9.	10.

ASSIGN THE PRIMARY

5.

1.	2.	3.	4.	5.
W			**W**	
6.	7.	8.	9.	10.

6.

		W		
1.	2.	3.	4.	5.
		W		
6.	7.	8.	9.	10.

7.

W				**W**
1.	2.	3.	4.	5.
W	**W**		**W**	
6.	7.	8.	9.	10.

8.

W	**W**	**W**	**W**	**W**
1.	2.	3.	4.	5.
W	**W**			
6.	7.	8.	9.	10.

ASSIGN THE PRIMARY

9.

W 1.	W 2.	W 3.	W 4.	W 5.
W 6.	W 7.	W 8.	W 9.	W 10.

10.

1.	2.	3.	4.	W 5.
W 6.	7.	W 8.	W 9.	10.

What is the primary if whorls appear in the following squares?

1. 1, 3, 4, 6, 7   1.
2. 1, 4, 5, 7, 8   2.
3. 1, 2, 3, 4, 7, 9   3.
4. 2, 4, 5, 7, 8, 9   4.
5. 2, 3, 5, 7, 8   5.
6. 2, 4, 6, 10   6.
7. 3, 4, 5, 6, 9   7.
8. 3, 5, 6, 7, 9   8.
9. 3, 6, 7, 8   9.
10. 4, 5, 6, 7, 10   10.

Give the Primary Classification

1. <u>W   W   W   U   W</u>   =
       U   W   W   W   U

2. <u>U   U   U   W   U</u>   =
       U   U   W   U   U

3. <u>U   W   U   U   U</u>   =
       W   W   U   U   U

4. <u>A   W   R   R   T</u>   =
       W   U   U   R   U

5. <u>U   U   U   U   U</u>   =
       W   W   W   R   W

6. <u>W   W   U   R   W</u>   =
       U   W   U   W   W

7. <u>U   U   R   W   W</u>   =
       W   W   U   W   U

8. <u>U   R   W   R   R</u>   =
       W   W   W   U   W

9. <u>A   A   R   U   W</u>   =
       U   U   U   U   U

10. <u>W   U   U   R   U</u>   =
       W   U   U   U   U

EXAMPLE FOR CLASSROOM PRACTICE

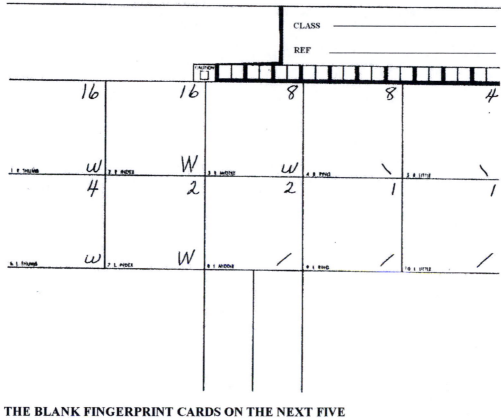

**THE BLANK FINGERPRINT CARDS ON THE NEXT FIVE
PAGES MAY BE USED FOR CLASSROOM PRACTICE**

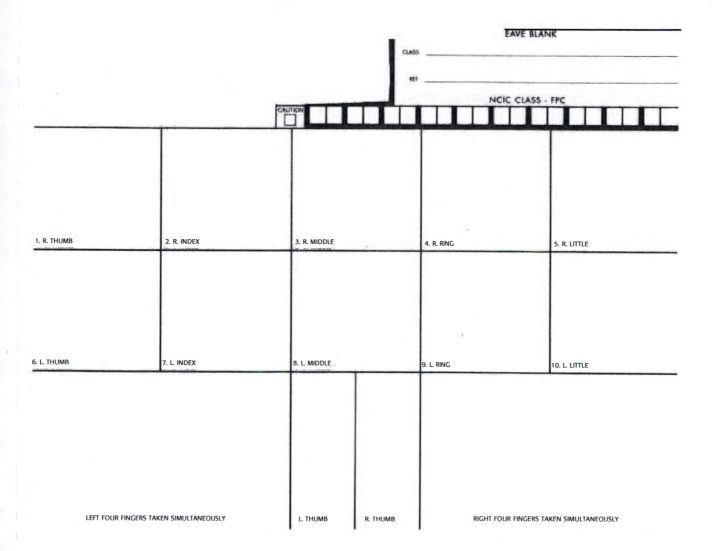

1

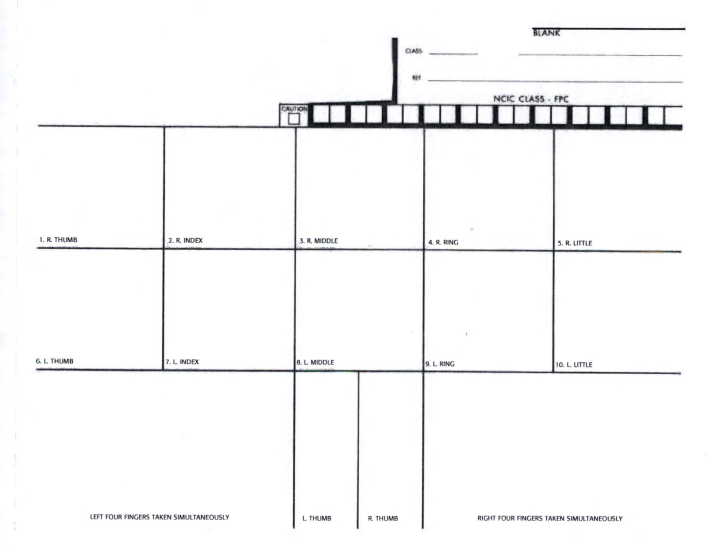

BLANK

CLASS _____

REF _____

NCIC CLASS - FPC

| CAUTION | | | | | | | | | | | | | | | | | | | | | |

| 1. R. THUMB | 2. R. INDEX | 3. R. MIDDLE | 4. R. RING | 5. R. LITTLE |

| 6. L. THUMB | 7. L. INDEX | 8. L. MIDDLE | 9. L. RING | 10. L. LITTLE |

LEFT FOUR FINGERS TAKEN SIMULTANEOUSLY

L. THUMB   R. THUMB

RIGHT FOUR FINGERS TAKEN SIMULTANEOUSLY

2

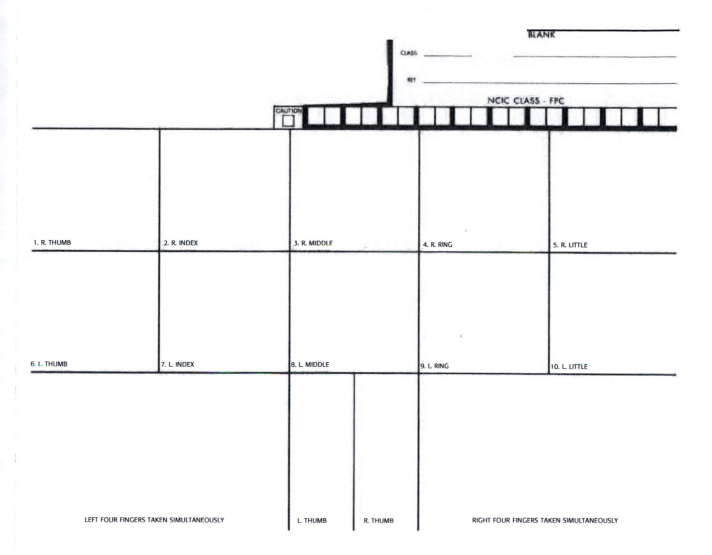

BLANK

CLASS

REF

NCIC CLASS - FPC

CAUTION

| 1. R. THUMB | 2. R. INDEX | 3. R. MIDDLE | 4. R. RING | 5. R. LITTLE |

| 6. L. THUMB | 7. L. INDEX | 8. L. MIDDLE | 9. L. RING | 10. L. LITTLE |

LEFT FOUR FINGERS TAKEN SIMULTANEOUSLY   L. THUMB   R. THUMB   RIGHT FOUR FINGERS TAKEN SIMULTANEOUSLY

3

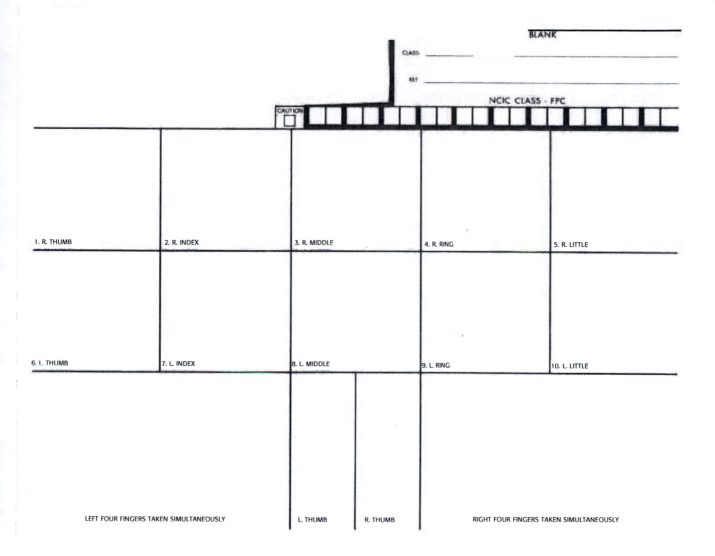

BLANK

CLASS

REF

NCIC CLASS - FPC

CAUTION

1. R. THUMB	2. R. INDEX	3. R. MIDDLE	4. R. RING	5. R. LITTLE
6. L. THUMB	7. L. INDEX	8. L. MIDDLE	9. L. RING	10. L. LITTLE

LEFT FOUR FINGERS TAKEN SIMULTANEOUSLY   L. THUMB   R. THUMB   RIGHT FOUR FINGERS TAKEN SIMULTANEOUSLY

4

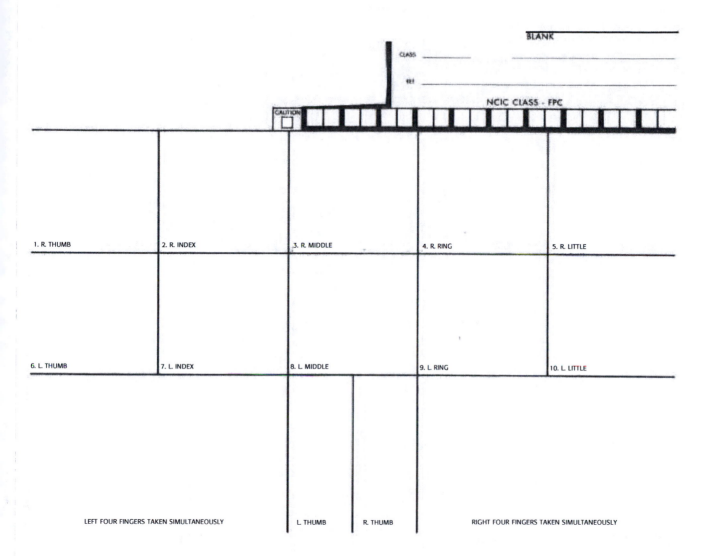

BLANK

CLASS

REF

NCIC CLASS - FPC

CAUTION

| 1. R. THUMB | 2. R. INDEX | 3. R. MIDDLE | 4. R. RING | 5. R. LITTLE |

| 6. L. THUMB | 7. L. INDEX | 8. L. MIDDLE | 9. L. RING | 10. L. LITTLE |

LEFT FOUR FINGERS TAKEN SIMULTANEOUSLY

L. THUMB   R. THUMB

RIGHT FOUR FINGERS TAKEN SIMULTANEOUSLY

5

CLASSIFICATION EXERCISE 1

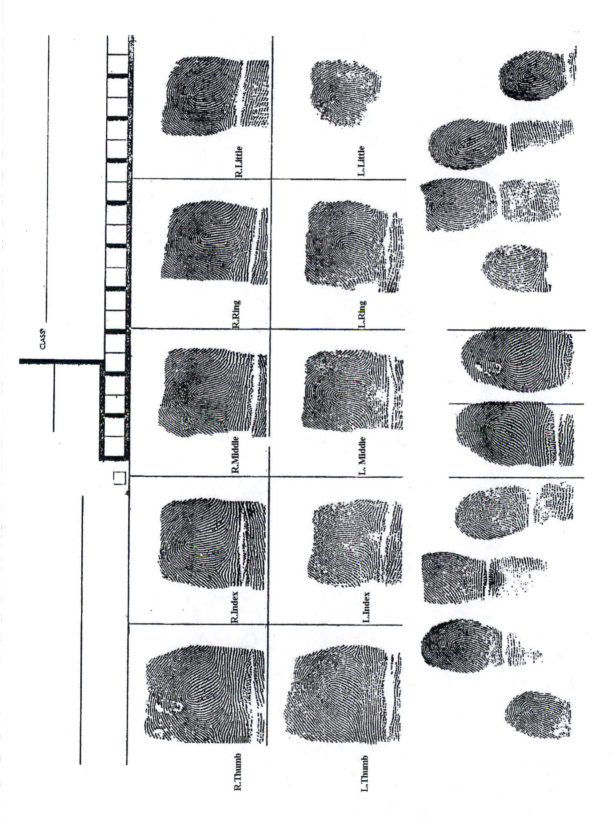

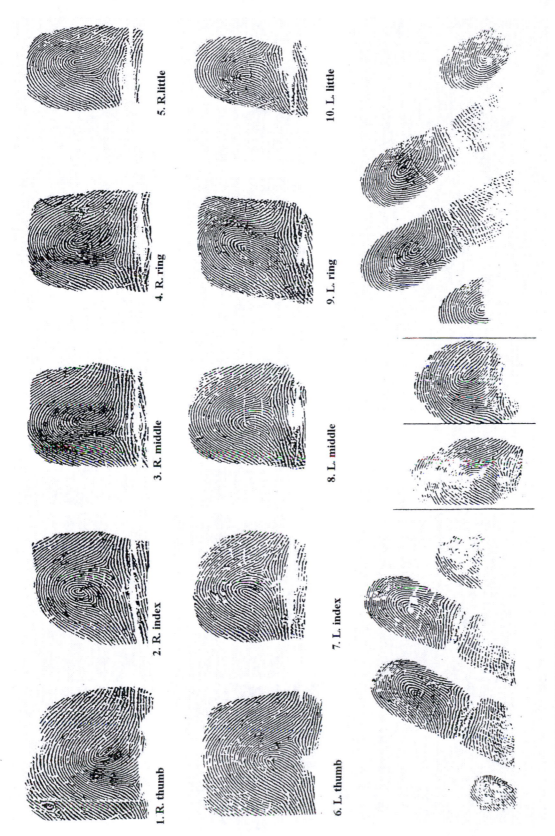

5. R.little

10. L. little

4. R. ring

9. L. ring

3. R. middle

8. L. middle

2. R. index

7. L. index

1. R. thumb

6. L. thumb

CLASSIFICATION EXERCISE 2

CLASSIFICATION EXERCISE 3

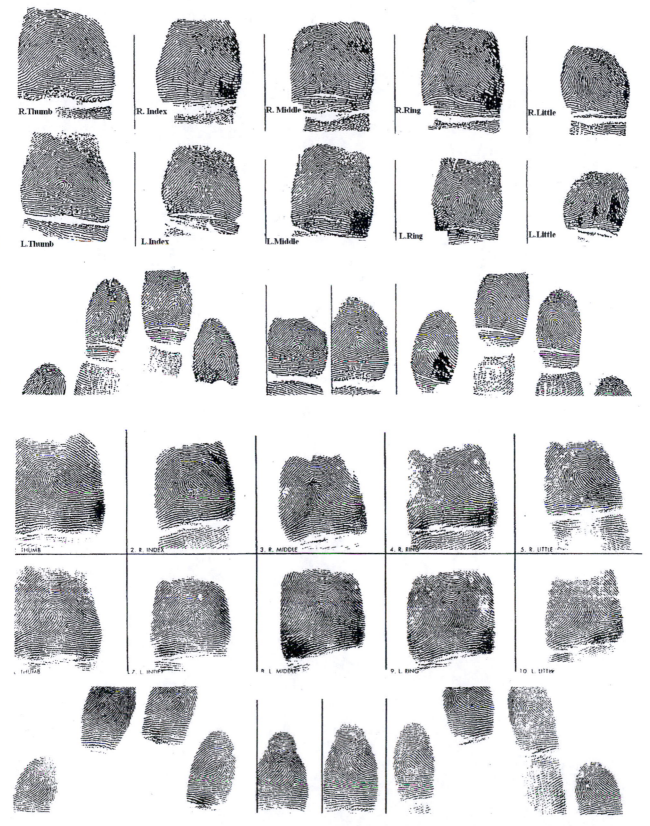

R.Thumb R. Index R. Middle R.Ring R.Little

L.Thumb L.Index L.Middle L.Ring L.Little

THUMB 2. R. INDEX 3. R. MIDDLE 4. R. RING 5. R. LITTLE

THUMB 7. L. INDEX 8. L. MIDDLE 9. L. RING 10. L. LITTLE

CLASSIFICATION EXERCISE 4

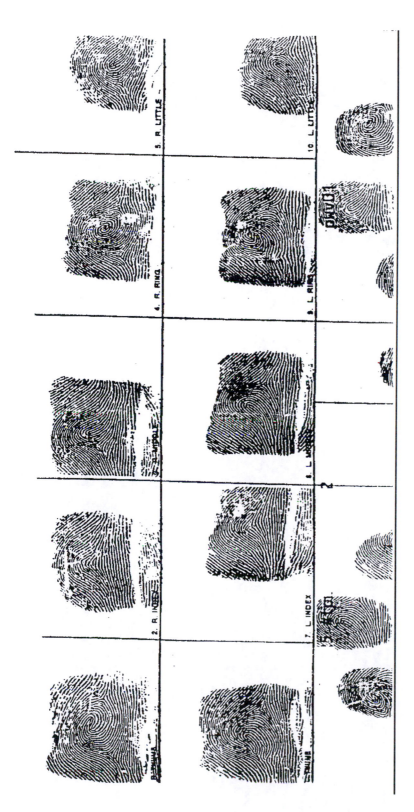

CLASSIFICATION EXERCISE 5

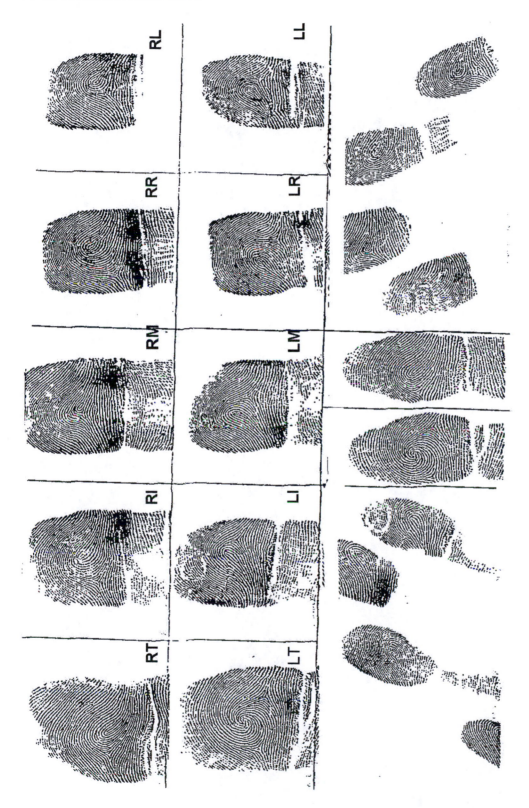

CLASSIFICATION EXERCISE 6

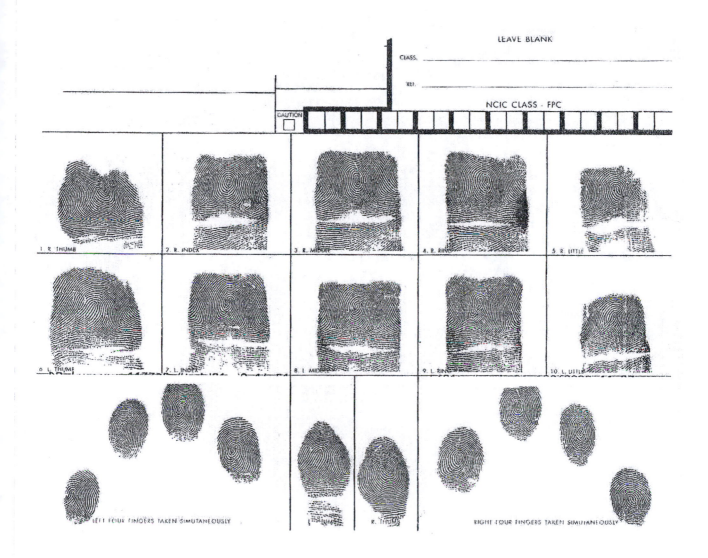

CLASSIFICATION EXERCISES 7 AND 8

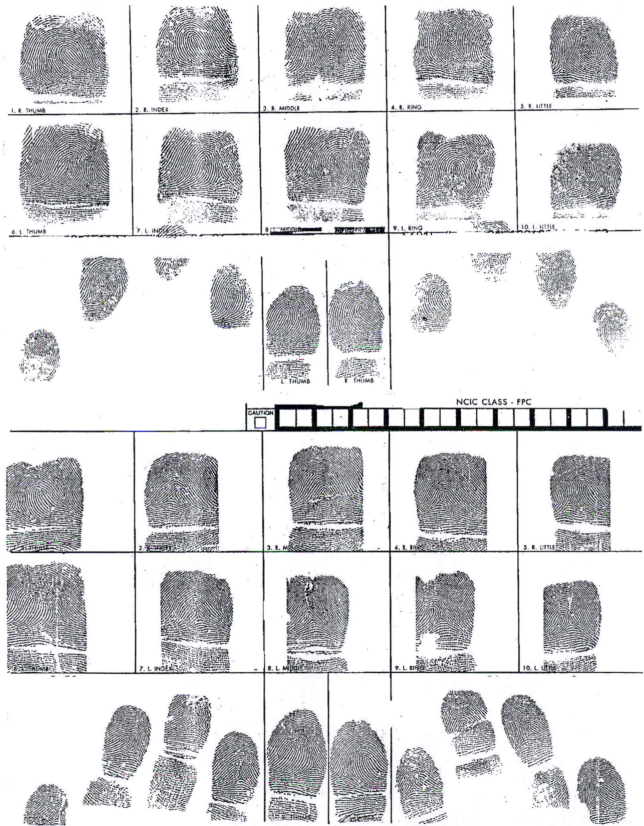

CLASSIFICATION EXERCISE 9

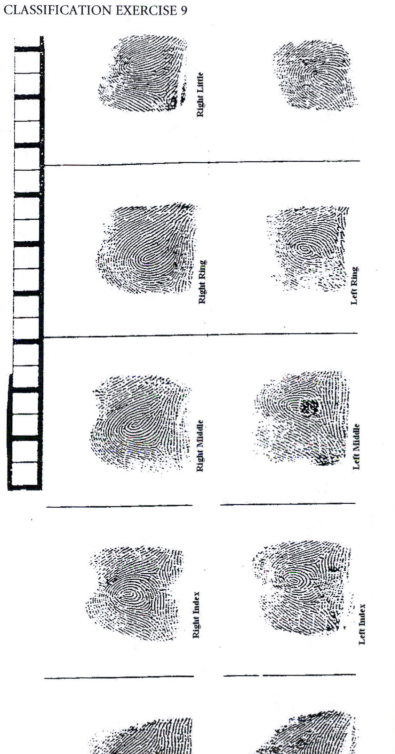

IDENTIFY THE DIVISION EACH PATTERN BELONGS TO
FOR EXAMPLE: (Ulnar, Radial, Plain, Central pocket loop, etc).

1.   2.   3.   4.   5.

6.   7.   8.   9.   10.

CLASSIFICATION EXERCISE 10—ASSIGN NCIC

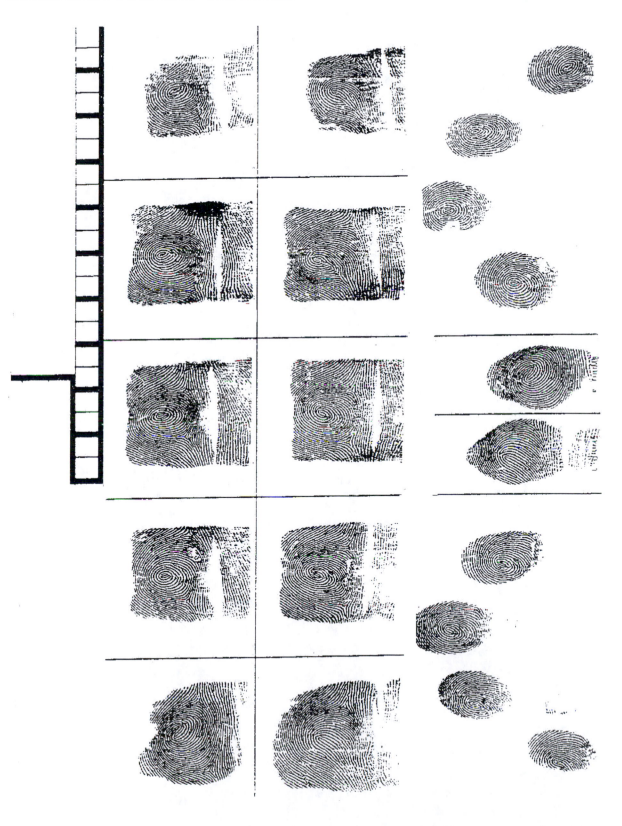

CLASSIFICATION EXERCISES 11 AND 12

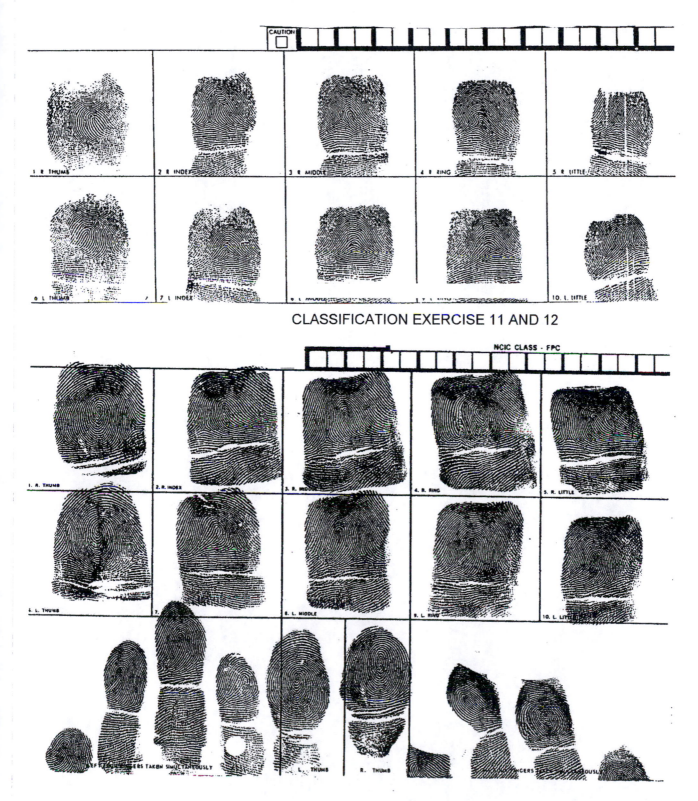

CLASSIFICATION EXERCISE 11 AND 12

CLASSIFICATION EXERCISES 13 AND 14

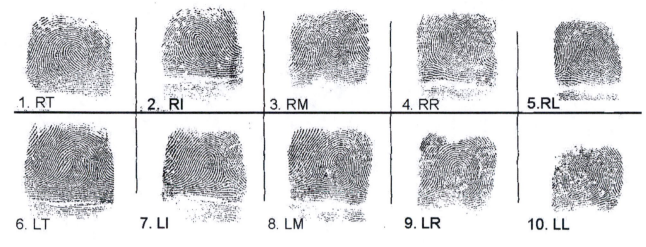

| 1. RT | 2. RI | 3. RM | 4. RR | 5.RL |
| 6. LT | 7. LI | 8. LM | 9. LR | 10. LL |

FINGER BLOCKS 1-10 REPRESENT THE SAME FINGERS AS SHOWN ABOVE

| 1. | 2. | 3. | 4. | 5. |
| 6. | 7. | 8. | 9. | 10. |

CLASSIFICATION EXERCISE 15

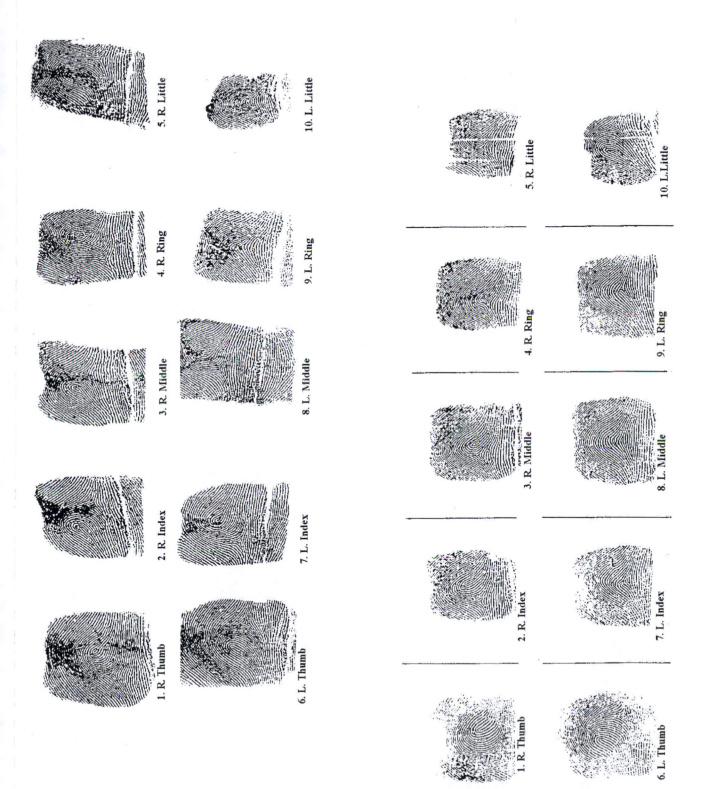

CLASSIFICATION EXERCISE 16

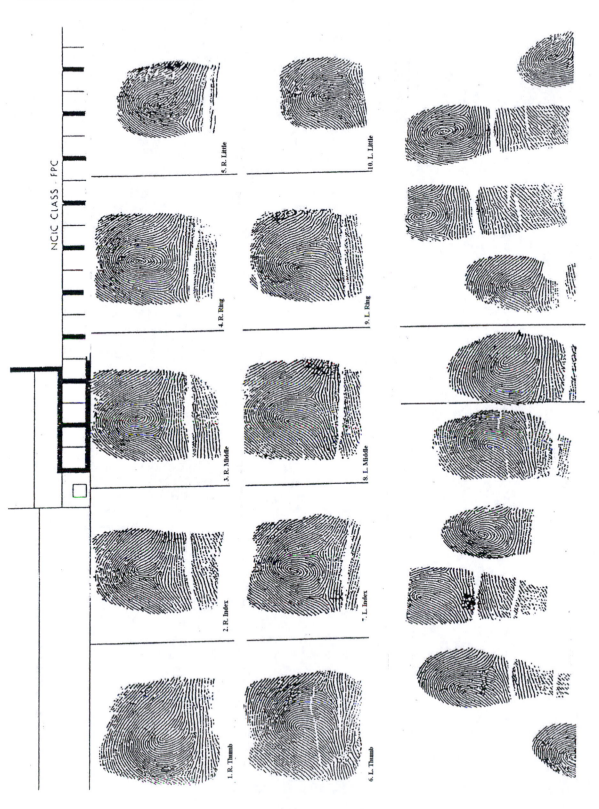

NCIC CLASS . FPC

1. R. Thumb
2. R. Index
3. R. Middle
4. R. Ring
5. R. Little
6. L. Thumb
7. L. Index
8. L. Middle
9. L. Ring
10. L. Little

CLASSIFICATION EXERCISE 17

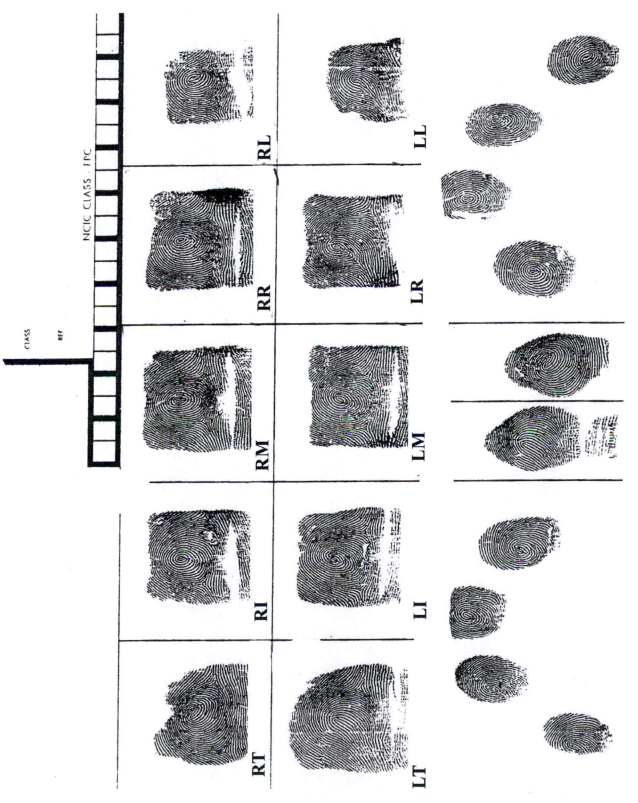

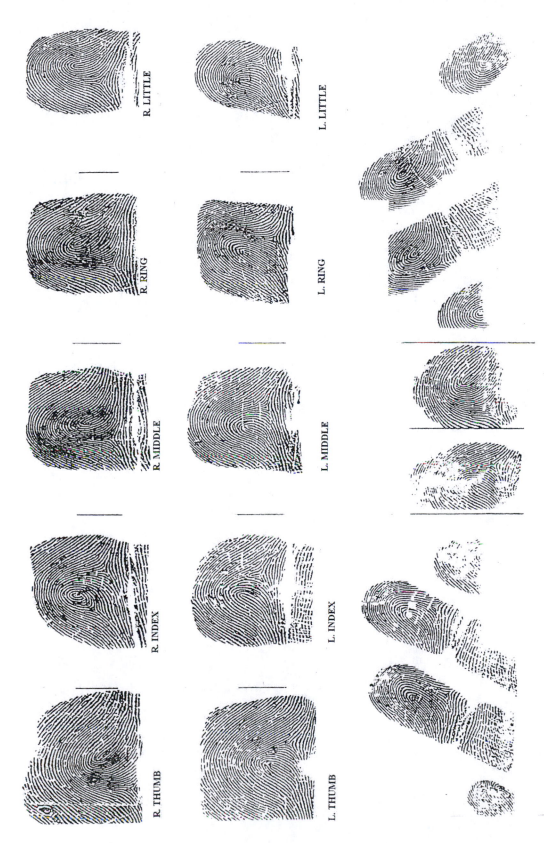

CLASSIFICATION EXERCISE 19

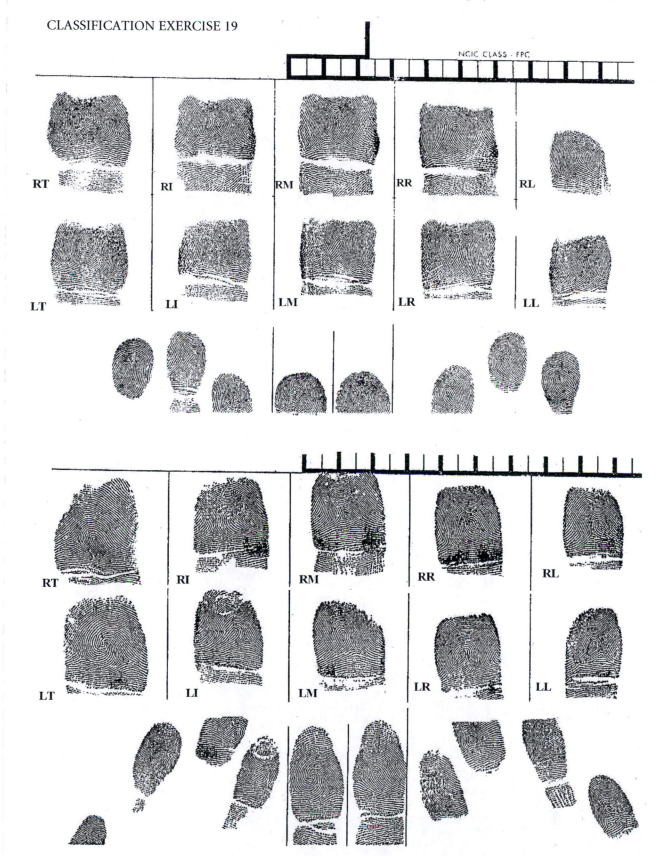

CLASSIFICATION EXERCISE 20

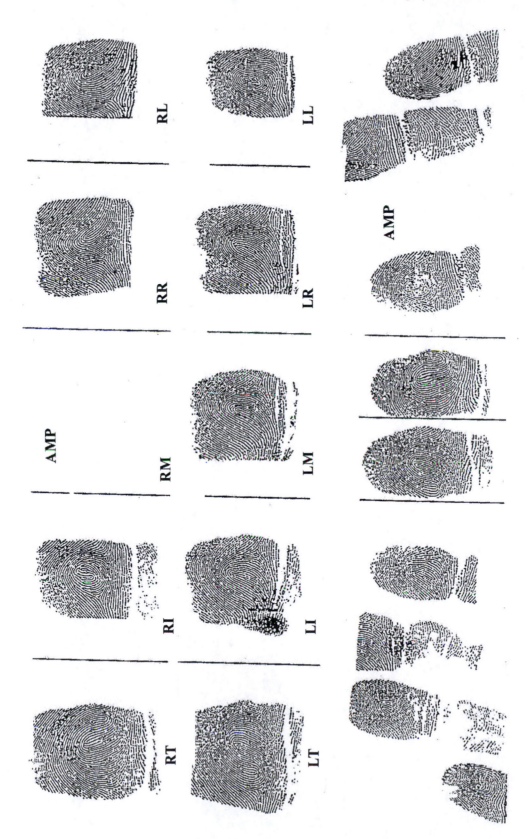

RL

LL

RR

LR

AMP

AMP

RM

LM

RI

LI

RT

LT

ASSIGN OPPOSITE PATTERN TO
AMPUTATED FINGER

SMALL LETTER CLASSIFICATION A AND B

A

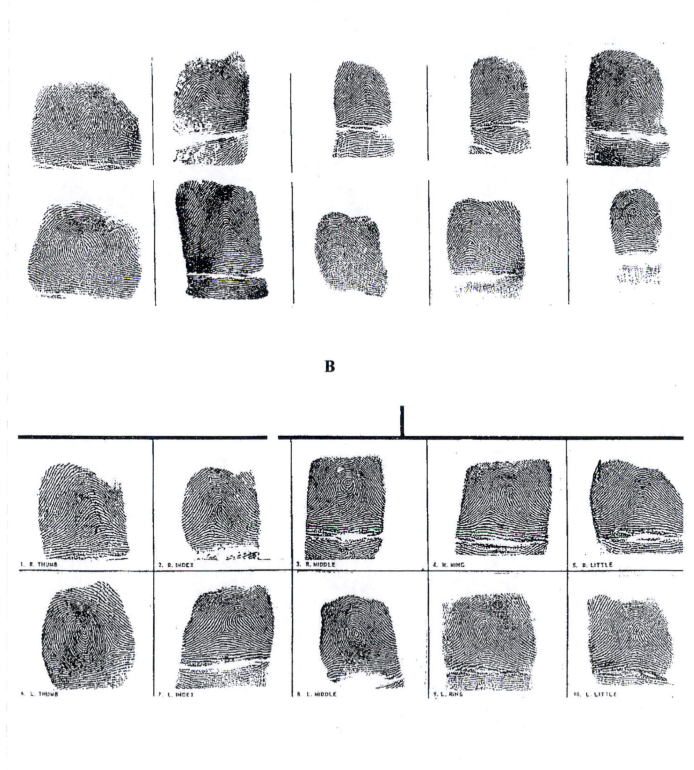

B

1. R. THUMB   2. R. INDEX   3. R. MIDDLE   4. R. RING   5. R. LITTLE

6. L. THUMB   7. L. INDEX   8. L. MIDDLE   9. L. RING   10. L. LITTLE

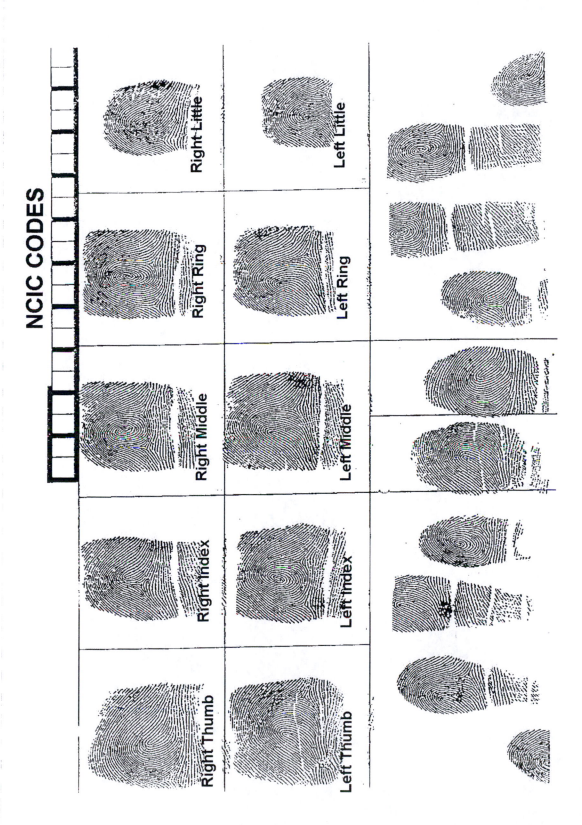

NCIC CODES

Right Thumb · Right Index · Right Middle · Right Ring · Right-Little

Left Thumb · Left Index · Left Middle · Left Ring · Left Little

PLACE RIDGE COUNTS OR WHORL TRACING IN THE UPPER RIGHT HAND CORNER OF EACH FINGER BLOCK

FINAL REVIEW - Page 1

TRUE OR FALSE

1. Fingerprints are distinctive ridge-outlines which appear on the outside of the end joints of the fingers and thumbs.
2. For classification and identification purposes, only the ridges, or black lines are considered
3. A bifurcation is two ridges splitting or forking into three or more branches.
4. Focal points are enclosed with the pattern area of arches.
5. The line of count is the imaginary line connecting the delta and the core.
6. Neither delta nor core is included in the ridge count.
7. Type lines are not always two continuous ridges.
8. The delta is the point at which the ridge count begins, but the delta is not included in the ridge count
9. The radial loop is a loop which flows toward the thumb.
10. A ridge count begins from the core and goes to the delta.
11. Both sides of an island are counted if the imaginary line from delta to core is crossed by them.
12. There are only three types of whorls.
13. In order to trace a whorl, it is first necessary to locate the deltas.
14. The ulnar loop is a loop which flows toward the thumb.
15. "Meeting whorl" means that the ridge being traced meets the right delta without crossing the circuits.
16. The delta must be placed on a ridge at or nearest the center of the divergence of the type lines.
17. When there are no rods inside the innermost recurve, the core is placed on the shoulder closest to the delta.
18. A white space must intervene between the delta and core in order to begin ridge counting.
19. Arches constitute about 65% of all fingerprint patterns.
20. The requirements for a loop type tented arch are: a sufficient recurve, a delta, and a ridge count across a looping ridge.
21. When a line drawn between the two deltas of a whorl touches one of the recurves, the whorl is considered a plain whorl.
22. The three tracings of a whorl are: meet, inside, and outer.
23. The term rod refers to the lines inside a recurve and may be used to determine the core.
24. The accidental whorl pattern will always have three deltas.
25. An appendage is located on the outside of the shoulders of a looping ridge.

FINAL REVIEW - Page 2

26. The type of pattern which has at least two deltas and a recurve in front of each is
    (a) central pocket (b) the pattern (c) whorl (d) accidental
27. The term impression refers to
    (a) ridges (b) whorls only (c) loops only (d) none of these
28. A whorl may be
    (a) spiral (b) circular (c) oval (d) all of these
29. The imaginary line in ridge counting is drawn from delta to
    (a) ridge (b) type line (c) bifurcation (d) core
30. The recurving ridges that are touched and considered in determining
    a plain or central pocket loop whorl are:
    (a) in front of the delta (b) between the two deltas
    (c) neither of these
31. The number of fingers involved in the subsecondary are:
    (a) two (b) three (c) five (d) six
32. A whorl has :
    (a) two circuits (b) two angles (c) two deltas
33. Whorl patterns in both thumbs will result in a primary of:
    (a) 5/17 (b) 1/3 (c) 17/1 (d) 23/17
34. In ridge counting, if the imaginary line crosses an island
    the areas counted are:
    (a) both sides (b) one side (c) the ridge below (d) none of the above
35. Ulnar loops flow toward
    (a) index finger (b) little finger (c) thumb (d) ring finger
36. 65% of all patterns are:
    (a) arches (b) loops (c) whorls (d) tented arches
37. The key is the ridge count of:
    (a) the little finger (b) both thumbs (c) first loop except little finger
38. In a plain whorl pattern, a line drawn between the two deltas
    must touch or cross :
    (a) the core (b) one delta (c) a recurving ridge within the
    pattern area (d) every recurve
39. There are three types of tented arches:
    (a) plain, upthrust, loop type (b) radial, loop type, angle
    ©_upthrust, loop, angle (d) none of the above
40. Whorl tracing begins at:
    (a) extreme left delta (b) right delta (c) type lines (d) recurve

FINAL REVIEW - Page 3

What is the sub-secondary for this set of prints?
(a) OOI   (b) I I I (c) MSI   (d) O I I
    IOI   IMI   IOI   OOO

1.	I w	2.	12 \	3.	9 \	4.	I w	5.	O w
6.	M w	7.	15 /	8.	13 /	9.	22 /	10.	4 /

Assign the Henry classification formula

1.	8 \	2.	I W	3.	13 \	4.	15 \	5.	4 \
6.	19 /	7.	O W	8.	18 /	9.	M w	10.	12 /

The following set of prints has: (a) no major (b) major of I/A (c) major of W/A
(d) major of I/a

1.	I w	2.	M W	3.	O w	4.	12 \	5.	a
6.	a	7.	T	8.	O w	9.	9 /	10.	10 /

An error has been made in blocking out this card: (a) patterns not traced (b) no
ridge counts © capitals not
shown (d)   all of the above

1.	w	2.	w	3.	w	4.	w	5.	w
6.	w	7.	w	8.	w	9.	w	10.	w

FINAL REVIEW - Page 4

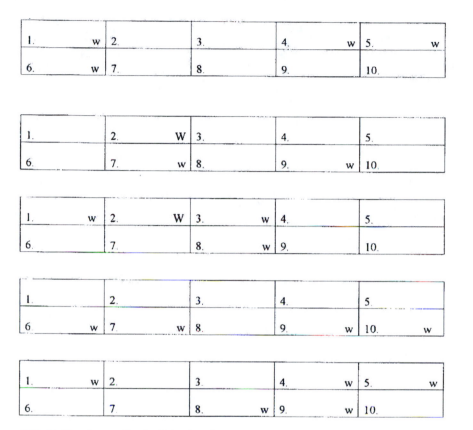

1. w	2.	3.	4. w	5. w
6. w	7.	8.	9.	10.

1.	2. W	3.	4.	5.
6.	7. w	8.	9. w	10.

1. w	2. W	3. w	4.	5.
6.	7.	8. w	9.	10.

1.	2.	3.	4.	5.
6. w	7. w	8.	9. w	10. w

1. w	2.	3.	4. w	5. w
6.	7.	8. w	9. w	10.

What is the primary of each of the above?

1.

2.

3.

4.

5.

FINGERPRINT COMPARISONS
Compare prints on this page to those shown on Page 2

1._____

2._____

3._____

4._____

5._____

6._____

7._____

8._____

9._____

10._____

FINGERPRINT COMPARISONS - PAGE 2

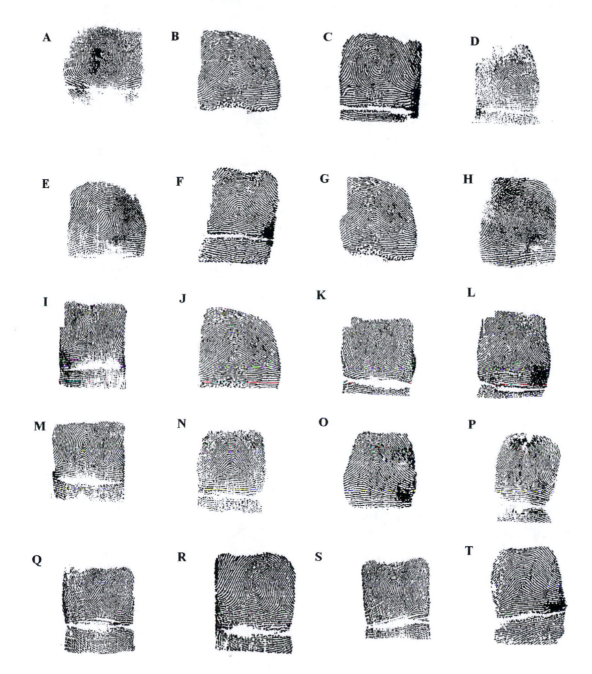